WARRIORS

OPERATION IRAQI FREEDOM 2005
3RD PLT ALPHA CO 4TH AAV
3/25 LIMA CO

JASON TEED

PALMETTO
P U B L I S H I N G
Charleston, SC
www.PalmettoPublishing.com

Hardcover ISBN: 978-1-64990-805-6
Paperback ISBN: 978-1-64990-649-6

TABLE OF CONTENTS

Introduction ·1
Our Arrival ·7
Operation River Bridge ·9
This Dam Life ·15
Operation Outer Banks ·19
QRF at Haditha Hospital ·31
Operation Matador ·38
Davis and Cole's Mortar ·54
311's IED ·59
Operation New Market ·65
Humvee on Grizzlies ·70
Operation Spear ·74
The Op That Never Happened ·82
Operation Sword ·84
Operation Sabre ·96
Operation Quick Strike ·104
Retrograde ·114
Life After Combat ·116
What does it mean to be a Veteran? · · · · · · · · · · · · · · · · · ·126
All Gave Some, 48 Gave All ·133

INTRODUCTION

More times than not when you hear about war stories from Iraq or Afghanistan its usually about some kind of special forces unit revolving around one incident or battle that happened to them while they were deployed. Not taking anything away from those guys because they're freaking amazing warriors and deserve all the credit given to them. But rarely do you hear stories about the line companies, the grunts. The warriors that go after it day after day kicking in doors, sweeping for IEDs, capturing detainees after detainees, clearing the cities of insurgents. The ones who endure months and months of a constant grind running on little to no sleep, little to no food, sweating their asses off op after op praying that today isn't their last day but accepting the fact that it very well could be. This book is dedicated to the ordinary men who did extraordinary things. Without these men going into the shit hole combat cities flushing out the insurgents, there could be no victories over there. We're the true backbone of the US military.

My main purpose in writing this book is to tell the story of our Marine Company who went in Iraq in 2005. 3rd Plt. Alpha Co. 4th AAV along with 3/25 Lima Company. Our deployment was 7 months of pure hell. In that time 48 Marines gave their lives for our great country. I wanted to honor those warriors and to keep their spirits alive so they will never be forgotten. As well as honoring those of us who survived. We went through so many hard times and did so many amazing things, I feel like many others can relate to our story. Which brings me to the second purpose in writing this book, our life afterwards. My hope is that at least one person will read this and understand that they are not alone. That what we went through is not normal, but what we're going through now IS normal. And hopefully itll be enough to jumpstart a change in their life for the better. Im going to share my personal experiences and things that ive done to help pull me out of my low points. If only one person takes something positive away from this, then its all worth it for me. You are not alone brothers.

In this book you will probably find horribly misspelled words, terrible structure, commas where there shouldn't be one, and long ass sentences because I don't know how to end them correctly. Lets face it, im not educated. I graduated at the University of Al Anbar Province in Iraq and I promise you grammar wasn't my major there. But what you will find in this book are honest words from one Marine who was there, spoken straight from the heart. Im going to lay it all out, good and bad. This is not going to be an easy book to write, but I feel like our story needs to be heard. This book is mostly based on my own experiences seen through my eyes, along with a journal that I kept while I was there. Ill also be obtaining stories from a few other Marines that was there as well. It's a story about one amtrac platoon that was a part of one of the hardest hit Marine Company in the Iraq war. This is the way we saw it and remember it. Also there wont be any political correctness here either. I'll be continuously referring to the insurgents as fuckers, goat fuckers, and Muj mother fuckers throughout the book. So If any of you snowflakes have a problem with that, I don't care.

My unit was 3rd Plt Alpha Co. 4th AAV. Amtrackers YAT-YAS. An amtrac is basically an oversized tank that carries the infantry in the back. Troop transport. We've all seen the commercials and movies where the vehicle pulls up, drops the back ramp down, and the grunts run out the back. Well that's basically an amtrac.. Our unit was deployed twice while I was in the unit. In 2003 we carried 3/1 Kilo Co. during the initial push from Kuwait to Baghdad. And at one point we were the farthest north Marine Company leading the way. We got in many firefights there and saw more dead bodies than I care to remember. 30

days of balls to the wall in a combat convoy, each day having maybe 1 meal, 1 water bottle, and if we were lucky 1-2 hours of sleep. 30 days of no shower, and when I finally did it was standing butt naked in Sadaam's kitchen dumping water over my head from a cup. And I felt like a million dollars after that shower too. But all that is a whole nother story. This book is about our 2005 deployment. We attached to 3/25 Lima Co., a reserve infantry unit out of Ohio. The way it works in the Marine Corps, when an infantry unit deploys all of the attachments that go with them become that infantry unit too. So when my unit 3rd Plt A Co 4th AAV deployed with 3/25 grunts, we became 3/25 ourselves for the time we were there. Same goes for Tankers, Snipers, Weapons, etc. Roughly 220 Marines in total. So for the remainder of this book, when I refer to 3/25 Lima im talking about all of us, not just specifically the grunts.

3/25 was deployed from February - October 2005 to Al Anbar Province western Iraq. Our area of operation was everything northwest of Ramadi from a town called Hit all the way to the Syrian border. We called it the Wild West. Our mission was very simple, flush out the insurgents from the cities. Search and destroy. The insurgents we were fighting was called the Mujahideen (we called them Muj, sounds like mooj). When we got there, all the little cities along the Euphrates River had virtually been untouched by Americans since the beginning of the war, with the exception of a few ops in and out of Haditha area. The Marines before us did a hell of a job in Fallujah, but while that was going on the cities northwest of that was steadily being imbedded with the Muj flooding in from Syria. The insurgents essentially ruled the cities. They terrorized the people constantly threatening them to not speak to us or give out any information. And if one person didn't comply with them, they would take them and the entire family and behead them. The civilians were scared to death of these fuckers. The insurgents setup IED factories, car bomb factories, and countless weapons caches all over. So when we got there, they had already fortified themselves within the cities waiting on us. Basically we were there to stir up the hornets' nest. And that's where this story begins.........

Side Notes

Before telling this story, I need to explain a few things so that its easier to follow. First of all, the vehicle that I operated is called an Amtrac, trac for short. (AAVP7A1). It's basically a troop carrier vehicle. Our tracs are like a tank, but were not nearly as armored as a tank. Our vehicles were designed to drive off the back of a ship in the ocean, and float like a boat to the shore, then drive on land to wherever our grunts needed to go to bring them to the fight. The back ramp drops down and the grunts run out, just like you see in the movies. We used those vehicles in Iraq to bring our infantry to the towns, drop them off so they could clear houses, and follow along side of them to provide support. We would drive next to them on the city roads guarding them from any oncoming threat. We could resupply their food, water, and ammo. We would haul out detainees or captured weapons out of the city, we could set up a road block whenever needed, and of course we had heavy machine guns for fire support. We have a M-2 .50cal machine gun and a MK19 grenade launcher mounted in a turret for our big guns. Our vehicles weren't really designed for this kind of use, but its what we had at the time so we made the best of it.

3rd Platoon (my platoon) consisted of 12 amtracs. One platoon of tracs carry one company of grunts. (infantry is referred to as grunts). So we break our platoon down into three sections. 1st section tracs carried 1st platoon grunts. 2nd section tracs carried 2nd platoon grunts. And of course 3rd section tracs carried 3rd platoon grunts. As I said before our grunts were 3/25 Lima Company. Lima company was labeled the main effort line company. So for the most part every operation the battalion did, Lima Company was always the company pushing in the cities. So of course that meant my platoon was the main effort as well. Every other company in the battalion for the most part provided support for us.

Lima Company was staged at Haditha Dam. This was our FOB (forward operating base). Haditha Dam is a hydroelectric dam just north of the city Haditha on the Euphrates River. We did all our operations out of this place. We actually lived inside the dam. The food sucked, the showers sucked, bathrooms were porto-cans, but at least we could sleep somewhat peacefully in a place that protected us from mortars. There was about 10,000,000 steps to the top of the dam. And of course that's where the food and phones were. The phone setup was horrible. You would wait hours for a 20 minute call, and that's if you could get in touch with someone. Also that's if the phones were even working that day. Our room was on the third floor inside the dam. It was a big open room full of bunk beds. Our tracs were staged at the foot of the dam. When we weren't doing ops, we would be out there working on the vehicles.

A few terms that you will frequently see in this book:

IED – improvised explosive device

SVBIED – suicidal vehicle borne improvised explosive device (car bomb)

OP – operation

Grunts – infantry

Tracs – amtracs

KIA – killed in action

WIA – wounded in action

FOB – forward operating base

QRF – quick reaction force

OUR ARRIVAL

Our platon was activated in december of 2004. We had a little bit of time to get our affairs in order before deploying and on January 4, 2005 we left for Camp Lejeune, North Carolina. We stayed there for a couple months to train for the deployment. Since we're an amtrac platoon we mostly focused on doing urban combat training, room to room type stuff. It was a long two months and the weather sucked, but we got through it. On March 13th Gulfport 3rd platoon left for Iraq. We flew into Kuwait airport and from there we hopped on a C-130 and flew into Al Asad, Iraq. Al Asad is an air base that we took over in 2003. This place is about as close to America as you can get in Iraq. They had Burger King, Pizza Hut, Subway, phone centers, gyms to workout, etc. Of course that's not where we got to stay, we still had to travel to the arm pit of Iraq, Haditha Dam. Our tracs were at the dam, so we had to wait for a convoy to come pick us up and bring us there. But, the convoy that was coming hit an IED on the way to pick us up. Right then we realized that this was going to be a rough deployment. I remember Sgt Woullard gathered us up and led us in a prayer for our protection for the next several months. A very touching moment, and very fitting for the deployment we were about to face. Finally on the night of March 17, we arrived at Haditha Dam. At first, I was impressed. Its this huge concrete structure in the middle of the desert that can be seen for miles and miles away. Then I remember thinking to myself, "why the hell are we staying at a place that can be seen for miles and miles away." The following day we did a relief in place with the previous trac unit that was there. The vehicles needed a little bit of work so we spent the next few days busting ass to get them ready to roll. Within a weeks time we go from eating at Outback Steak House in North Carolina to combat effective - ready to op in Haditha Dam. 3/25 Lima had already made relief before we got there, so now all the pieces were in place for us to start doing operations. Our Battalion Commanding Officer had a hard on for winning the war. Which is a good thing. Otherwise what are we doing there? The plan was for us to have a high op tempo. Hit them hard, hit them fast, and hit them often. And in the next few days we received our first op order. Operation River Bridge.

OPERATION RIVER BRIDGE

15 MARCH 2005 – 26 MARCH 2005

Operation River Bridge was the first operation for 3/25 Lima. It was conducted from March 15-26. The purpose of this operation was to hit a few towns in the area and make our presence known. We of course were to find insurgents and weapons caches, but mostly to talk to the civilians one on one and get a general idea of whats going on in the cities. Since we were a little late getting to the Dam, our grunts actually started the op a few days before we got involved. On the 20th of March is when our tracs rolled out to link up with our grunts in the city Haditha.

When we arrived in the city we first went straight to where our grunts were to load them up. That's when we realized that we were also working with the ING. (Iraqi National Guard). The ING was basically a group of Iraqis that were tired of the insurgents flooding in and running their country. They wanted to fight and win their country back. I have all the respect in the world for these guys. So when we met up with our grunts, we loaded them up along with the ING and moved to another area to clear more houses. We spent the next couple days clearing the city. As the grunts would push forward clearing houses, we would stay along with them on the street providing security. The following afternoon we set up a FOB in the middle of the city. We were to settle in there for the night. As soon as we got there my section (3rd section) was called to be a QRF (quick reaction force) for some ING that had just hit an IED and was taking small arms fire. We rushed over there with 3 vehicles to help provide security for them and to load up the wounded and KIA and bring them back to the Dam. As soon as we arrived we loaded one of the wounded on my vehicle and the other wounded and KIAs on the other vehicles. While doing that, a tank shot their main gun and blew the fuck out of a nearby house that had just shot an RPG at us. Fun times. We hauled ass headed back to the Dam going straight through the middle of Haditha. This was the shortest route back to the Dam, but also the most dangerous. It didn't matter though because we had to rush these Iraqis to help as soon as possible. We were lucky and made it all the way back without any issues. As soon as we arrived there were two Blackhawk helos waiting to take the serious wounded away. We drove up, dropped the ramp, and unloaded them. There were about 10 docs there waiting to treat these people. We had two KIA, and four or five wounded. Two of which were helo'd out on the Blackhawks.

After all that chaos we headed back to our FOB in Haditha. We were supposed to go raid a house later that night, but it got postponed because that evening a Humvee hit a land mine nearby. We lost one Marine in that attack, Cpl. Richardson. I don't know much about what all happened, other than what we heard on the radio that they were hit, and he was taken away by other Humvees. So we went out to the site to recover any gear that the enemy could possibly get a hold of, including the radios, weapons, night vision, etc. All in all our first couple days in our first operation turned out to be pretty shitty. It definitely was not a good sign for things to come for us.

The next morning we left Haditha and headed straight to Haqlani-yah, another city further south. Not thirty minutes of being there an IED exploded on one of our 7-ton vehicles. The whole convoy passed over this thing first, and they decided to blow it on one of our trucks a few vehicles behind me. It was actually a relatively a small IED, so it didn't do much damage at all and everyone was ok. Ten minutes after that we had truck driving high speed straight towards us. I just happened to be looking in that direction at the time so I saw the whole thing. It was an SVBIED attack (suicide car bomb). But our Weapons Platoon shot and killed the driver before he was able to detonate on us. It was a truck carrying 400 gallons of gas that had a trigger for the driver to blow it. It all happened extremely fast, which was an eye opener for us that things could go to shit real fast if were not on our toes. Here we are only a few days in and we've been attacked multiple times. I guess since we were there making our presence known, they were attempting to do the same. It was definitely in the early stages for them. Their attacks became much larger and much more sophisticated. Just like we were testing their tactics, they were testing ours as well. One thing is for sure though, they were there to fight. So for us, that meant its go time! The next couple days were pretty quiet. We pushed through the rest of the city clearing houses and talking to the people. Finally once we finished clearing the city, we rolled out and headed back to the Dam.

Overall for our first op it was a big success, despite our wounded and KIA. We ended up finding over 100 RPG rounds, about 150 artillery rounds (used for IEDs), and a few detainees. Plus we made good contacts with the civilians there and explained what our goals were. Contrary to popular belief, the Iraqi civilians loved us. Especially the children. They all wanted us there to help take back their cities. But they were too scared to talk to us or help us in fear of what the insurgents would do to them if they found out. We knew right away It was going to be a very complex deployment.

25 March 2005
Cpl. Bryan J. Richardson

THIS DAM LIFE

Life at Haditha Dam was bullshit. It was forward operating base, so we didn't have all the luxuries that Al Asad air base had. The whole platoon stayed inside the Dam, in one big room with bunk beds. It was dark, and always damp because we were literally under water level and there was no moving air inside. We had to hand wash all of our clothes from a water spicket outside, we had to eat tray rats (basically one step above MRE's). Except for supper, we sometimes had actual fake meals, but it wasn't good. Our showers were small trailers with tiny stalls in it, for the entire Dam to use. Our bathrooms were Porto Shitters outside that never had toilet paper and were ALWAYS full. And every where you went inside the Dam you had to take 10 million stairs to get there. But we did receive a constant supply of mail. We were able to get packages of "Listerine" bottles and have our whiskey nights. We had some of the best nights of our lives in that place. So despite all of the bad, we made the best of it because that's what Marines do, we adapt and overcome.

At the Dam we were mortared daily. They would usually come flying in groups of 3. Most of the time they were way off, but sometimes they would get close. Being that we were amtrackers, we were constantly outside working on our vehicles if we weren't on ops. So we were always around the mortar attacks. We would hear the pops from the launch and we would scatter taking cover in anything nearby. Then afterwards we would go back to work as if nothing happened. This was our life daily, sometimes twice a day. I remember one night I was trying to take a shower in the bullshit trailer outside, and all of a sudden we started getting mortared. Imagine a bunch of naked dudes running out of a shower to take cover inside the Dam. Not a pleasant sight by any means, but fucking hilarious though. Several times the rounds would land right on top of us. I'll cover more on that later on in this book, but definitely some hard days there.

Also we had a ton of Iraqi civilians that would come in every day to operate the Dam. It still was a functioning Dam that supplied power to a huge portion of Iraq. So we had to have someone maintaining it. The downside to that is we didn't know who to trust there. We knew that some of them were muj, so we had to constantly be on guard. We had to grow eyes in the back of our head. Even at night when we would sleep, we always had to have someone on watch incase one of those fuckers tried to do something stupid. So literally in the seven month deployment, between the ops and living in the Dam, there was NEVER a moment where we felt safe or at ease. That's a hard way to live for an extended period of time. I don't think I ever got a good nights sleep there. Always on edge, always. And that alone is enough to change a man.

All in all though it really wasn't a bad place to be considering we had a huge concrete structure we could take cover in. Even though it was a huge target for the enemy, we at least had some kind of a secure building. There were other places in Iraq like Camp Hit that had minimal secure structures and would get attacked regularly. So even though we didn't get so lucky to stay at the air base, I still felt somewhat lucky to have what we had. But definitely not a place I would ever want to vacation at or even see again. Fuck that place. The damn Dam, we loved it and hated it all at the same time.

OPERATION OUTER BANKS

01 APRIL 2005 – 01 MAY 2005

Operation Outer Banks was a month long operation that was actually broken up into several smaller operations. The plan was to hit most of the major cities along the Euphrates River south of the Dam. Our original objective was to clear out Barwahah, then move to the other side of the river and clear Baghdadi (not to be confused with Baghdad), Abu Hyat, Al Muhammadi, and Kubaysah. Basically the same thing as the last operation, clear the cities of insurgents and weapons caches, get to know the locals and explain why we're there, and gather intel. We left the Dam on April 1st with all of 3/25 Lima grunts, our platoon of tracs, tanks, and Weapons Company, and headed straight to Barwanah.

Once we arrived at Barwanah, the first couple days our tracs set up a blocking position on the roads keeping anyone from entering or exiting. While we were doing that Lima Co and Weapons Co moved into the city and started clearing. During that time we heard several firefights within the city. We knew Barwanah was a corrupt town because they had a concrete monument with a picture of Saddam still standing within the city. We knew it was an insurgent stronghold. After the first couple days we killed several insurgents and detained even more. After that we moved into the city where the Saddam picture was and set up a FOB there. We took over a school of somekind right along the Euphrates River. Within about 30 minutes of being there we started getting mor-

19

tared. A few rounds landed roughly 30 yards from our vehicles. The rounds were launched from across the river on Haqlaniyah side. We returned fire into the palm groves along the banks of the river from where they were mortaring from. Nobody was hurt during the attack, but after a few days of firefights and then this, we knew we had started stirring up something.

That afternoon we left Barwanah and went straight to the Dam for the night. We had to cross over the Euphrates River to hit the other cities so we decided to rest up for the night, well most of us did. I was having mechanical issues on my vehicle. So me and the mech John Carl Milioto stayed up all night working on it to get it up and running. And we did, until dawn when it was time to roll out again. That's the way it is sometimes in Iraq, you go for days with little to no sleep, but the mission comes first. At first light, we rolled out straight for Baghdadi, a town several hours south from where we were. On the way there 2nd section tracs broke off and went to Haditha Train Station. We had received intel that there was a huge weapons cache there. While clearing out the station, we started receiving small arms fire and eventually RPGs and mortars. My friend Bobby Davis's trac was hit with an RPG during that raid. The rod from the RPG went straight through the final drive of the trac and underneath Davis's legs. Overall about four grunts got wounded, gun shot wounds in the arms and legs, shrapnel to the face, even one of them had their teeth knocked out somehow. It was a hard hit but nobody was killed during that attack.

On the way to Baghdadi was a very long and tiring drive. But eventually we made it there and started to clear the city. Baghdadi was supposed to be another insurgent stronghold city, but when we got there it was pretty quiet. We pushed through the city pretty fast. We would see signs of enemy activity, like an Iraqi police station that was bombed to hell and back previously from the insurgents. But no activity out of the ordinary for us. We tried our hardest to draw out the enemy and make contact, we even stayed at the police station as a symbol that we're ready to throw down. But nothing happened in that town. It was quiet. I do believe we won the hearts and minds of the people though. We met a lot of nice Iraqi civilians, you could tell they wanted us there and loved us. Which is definitely something they wont show you on main stream media. I did buy me a turban from one of the locals, and a bag of Tek Tak Doom (which is basically an off brand of cheetos but disgusting).

We left from there and went to Abu Hyat. This was a very small dirt hut city. Absolutely no action in that city but we did find a few weapons caches there. No contact whatsoever. Actually it was pretty boring there, but hell ill take boring over getting ambushed anyday. We stayed there for a couple days and finally headed to Al Asad air base about an hour north. This was the Promised Land for us forward fighters. They had cokes, ice cream, and ice there. Ice is a luxury that unless you go without it for a long time you don't know how valuable it is, like a shower. And hot meals. Actual meals, not tray rations and MRE's like we've been getting at the Dam. We spent a few days there getting our tracs fixed up and kinks worked out so that we could op effectively again. During that time our grunts helo'd out for another op to clear the cities Al Muhammadi, and Kubaysah. Our plan was to link back up with them in a few days to hit the Haditha Train Station once again to recheck that area. We did that and pushed through the area, and found nothing. Afterwards headed back for the Dam, temporarily.

Roughly 20 minutes after pulling in the gates of the Dam, we started getting mortared. Someone from the outside was watching us for when we pulled in, and had our coordinates zeroed in on their mortar tubes. They were hitting about 50 yards away, which normally isn't much of a threat. But some shrapnel flew and hit my buddy Penzo directly in the balls. It grazed his sack, but didn't actually damage anything. That's about as lucky as it gets. Everytime I see him to this day I ask him how his nuts are. We stayed at the Dam for a couple days. And during that time we got word that the mayor of Haditha and all of his family was assassinated in the local soccer field. So the next day our section went straight to Haditha to investigate and try to draw the insurgents out. Once again they wouldn't fight, chicken shit bastards. A few days later we got a QRF (quick reaction force) call for our Weapons Company in Haqlaniyah. Apparently they were ambushed so we rushed out with the entire platoon of tracs to help out. Once we got there we were engaged a few times but nothing major. After that attack, we decided to add Haqlaniyah to the list of cities to clear during Operation Outer Banks.

We came back to the Dam to regroup and prepare for the op. During that time we got word that over 20 Iraqi police officers were assassinated in Haditha by the insurgents. At that point our company operation became a Battalion operation. Basically the entire Battalion would surround the cities while we would push through and clear Haqlaniyah. So on April 21st we pushed out to head straight for Haqlaniyah. Within the first day of clearing the city, we detained over 20 Muj, and found several weapons caches. We had a few engagements but nothing too serious. I remember that night driving out the detainees in my trac and handing them over to our command post. They were tied up and blind folded, crying their eyes out. Those fuckers were scared to death, which is good. Fuck them. They shouldn't have been a Muj mother fucker from the start. We continued through Haqlaniyah for the next few days, doing what we've been doing. Trying to find the bad guys. We had finally gotten to the end of the city. This was the tail end of Operation Outer Banks. We had taken over a large mansion where the old ambassador of the city used to live. We set in for the night and was planning to head back to the Dam in the morning. We got a call on the radio that our snipers were taking small arms fire and RPGs. My section hauled ass over there with 3 vehicles to counter attack. My vehicle was last in the line. We drove through the city and finally got to the ambush point, but there was nothing going on. The insurgents had fled and it was quiet. Now usually when its quiet like that, we're on the highest alert. There's alot of truth to that old saying "a little too quiet". The next thing we see is a car driving high speed headed straight to our convoy. It was driving at us from behind, which was straight at my vehicle. The snipers had shot a flare at it to warn them that we were there. Then my crew shot a few warning shots. The car kept coming. All of this happened in a few seconds. My guys looked at me for the word, and i gave them the only option i felt like we had. I said "Light em up!" And that's what we did. I didn't have enough time to spin the vehicle around and put the 50 cal on them. Plus the snipers were directly down range. So we put about a hundred rounds from of 5.56 in the car. We finally stopped the car about 30 yards from us. We ended up killing the driver and wounding the passenger. As it turned out, there was nothing in the car. We had been hearing reports all day about a suicide car bomb in the area. So when that happened i thought for sure that was it. Its a common tactic for the insurgents to draw us out with small arms fire, and then hit us with an IED or car bomb. When I saw that car heading full speed at us, i thought that was the end for us. It was a fucked up situation for us. As far as I know that wounded guy survived. It sucks that everything happened the way it did. I really have no idea why those guys drove at us like that. Especially after the flares and warning shots. Maybe they were insurgents testing us and learning our tactics. Maybe they were innocent civilians that were forced to drive at us by the insurgents.. Most likely they were just two people not paying attention. Who the hell knows. Even though I felt like we did the right thing, the fact that nothing was in the car really got to me. That was the end of Operation Outer Banks.

All in all it was a very successful operation. We ended up killing about 35 insurgents and detaining roughly 50. As well as finding dozens of weapons caches throughout the cities. We definitely put a dent in the Muj operations in that area. But still, we knew the rest of the deployment from that point on wouldn't be the same. After the multiple attacks and the assassinations, we knew the enemy was getting bolder and more aggressive. We knew we had stirred up the hornets. We knew it would only get harder.

13 April 2005
Cpl. Michael B. Lindemuth

26 April 2005
Cpl. Joseph S. Tremblay

QRF AT HADITHA HOSPITAL

07 MAY 2005

Right after our last op in Haditha and Haqlaniyah, first section tracs and our grunts headed up north to Al Qaim for a major op called Operation Matador. While they were gone, my section (third section) and second section tracs were left back to run all the day ops in and out of the dam. On the evening of May 7, 2005, 3rd section tracs was on standby for QRF (quick reaction force) for our mobile weapons unit KABAR, who had an op in Haditha that night. One of our other weapons units was across the river from Haditha earlier that day and reported receiving shots from Haditha side. So KABAR rolled out with a couple Humvees, a 7 ton truck, and a tank to counter attack where the shots were coming from. We were staged at the dam with our tracs and a few extra Marines that we had available ready to push out in case they ran into trouble.

Probably 15 minutes after KABAR left the dam, we heard a loud ass boom. KABAR unit had been ambushed at the Haditha hospital. Those fuckers fortified the hospital with sandbags waiting on us to come through. When they did they received small arms fire from the hospital and nearby houses. At that time a SBVIED (suicide car bomb) drove right into one of the Humvees. That was the boom we heard at the dam, roughly 6 miles away. As soon as we heard it, we rolled out to help. When we got there, it was pitch black with the only light coming from the burning Humvee and a fire from the hospital caused by the blast. I can still smell those smells today, the smell of spent explosives and the burning Humvee. When we pulled up we started receiving small arms fire We set into place and unloaded the makeshift grunt team so they could go in and clear the hospital. You could hear the firefight going on inside the hospital as well as shots from nearby houses. While they were doing that we were trying to recover the wounded and KIA from the ambush. It all seemed like pure chaos. Four Marines died from that IED. Three of those Marines were loaded up in the other Humvee and one Marine was loaded on my trac. Its one thing to see an enemy KIA, or even hundreds. But to see one of your own, its horrible. When I saw him it broke my heart. A million thoughts ran through my head. I thought about his family having to find this out the next day. He probably woke up that morning thinking it was a regular day and counting them down like all of us did. It sucks, bad. But all I could do is stay on watch in the turret and try to prevent something else bad from happening. After we loaded up the KIA and the grunts finished clearing the hospital, we rolled out of there. We were able to fight through the ambush and recover all of our Marines that night. No man left behind.

Once we got back we drove straight to the top of the dam where our medics were. They were expecting us there with the KIA so when we pulled up there was seemingly every corpsman from the dam outside waiting on us. We pulled up, shut the engine down, and dropped the ramp. I got out of the turret and into the back and I remember looking at the Marine. Just seeing what the IED did to him and seeing the blood soaked cammies, its an image that wont ever leave me. But what happened next is a moment ill never forget for the rest of my life. It was quiet, so quiet you could hear a pin drop. No one said a word. One of the corpsman walked onto the trac and grabbed the Marine's hand. He held it for a minute with his eyes closed as if he was praying or talking to him. It brought tears to my eyes, still does to this day. Afterwards, a few more corpsman came in and picked up the Marine and carried him off as if they were in dress uniform carrying a flag draped coffin. The rest of the corpsman out there stood aside and payed their respects as the Marine was carried inside the hospital. Again, no one said a word. It was a moment of pure respect and love, for a warrior who gave his life fighting for his brothers. I looked down at the Marines name and read "Graham", LCpl Lance T. Graham. I never met that man before that day, but not a day has gone by where I don't remember him.

Afterwards we went back down to the ramp where we parked our tracs. Me and Justin Adams tried to clean up the blood the best we could and get everything ready for the next day. We were supposed to go back to that spot and recover the remains of the Humvee. I don't think I slept at all that night. When the morning came we loaded up the same crew and vehicles and went back. It was early in the morning. Once we got there there was sparatic AK47 fire but nothing too bad. We finally could get a good look at what the blast did. It left a huge crater in the road and crumbled nearby houses and walls. Im not sure size of the IED but I would have to guess at least five or six 155mm artillery rounds. Big fucking blast. One of our tanks strapped the Humvee to the back and drug it out. My vehicle was second in the convoy heading back. About a half mile up the road an IED popped right in front of my vehicle. The blast was several meters out in front and didn't do any damage, so we pushed though it. Once we were passing the alley where the blast was we saw two muj mother fuckers running away who were the trigger men. So we all opened fire down the alley including Sgt David Hixon who was like John fucking Rambo on the M240. It was raining spent brass and we took them down. Shots fired in anger, there is no sweeter sound than that. And that sound never gets old. Once we gave those two goat fuckers their 72 virgins, we hauled ass again and all made it back to the dam.

After it was over they told us that we got our revenge on the ones who ambushed us. Im not sure how many we killed that night but we were told that there was blood all inside the buildings where they were shooting from. No matter how many of them we did kill, itll never replace the warriors we lost that night. God rest their souls. Semper Fi brothers.

07 May 2005
Sgt. Aaron N. Cepeda
Sgt. Michael A. Marzano
LCpl. Lance T. Graham
HM3 Jeffery L. Wiener

OPERATION MATADOR

04 MAY 2005 – 17 MAY 2005

Immediately following Operation Outer Banks, Lima Co along with a section of our tracs went up north to Al Qaim near the Syrian border. A major operation was in the works for Al Qaim, a major insurgent stronghold in northern Iraq. We knew that most of the insurgents were channeling from Syria through that city. So our objective was to eliminate the enemy staging areas there and north of the Euphrates River. This was one operation I was actually not a part of. Our 1st section of tracs went up there with all of Lima Co grunts to join up with 3/2 Marines, while the rest of our trac platoon stayed back at the Dam to do small ops in the area. Since I wasn't there I asked one of the greatest warriors that I know, Bryan Hillberg, for his accounts of that operation. So for this chapter, everything italicized is his story word for word, his heart poured out on paper.

"We had just got back from an Operation at the dam and were all chilling. I mean we hadn't been back 8 hours. The normal rhythm of weapon, gear, self was still going on. I had snuck up to the phone center to call home. I had just got the phone in my hand and someone came in and said "all Lima Marines OUT!!". I had no clue what was going on. Hoffman looked at me and said "this isnt good."

Next thing I know We were heading to Al Qaim. We got there and it was an ok base. Was some sort of old train station and had a badass chowhall. We stayed in transient barracks and were told that the higher ups needed a few days to solidify the plan. I have no idea how long we were really there. I do know we were briefed that this was NOT Haditha. ROEs had changed. 100 yd buffers before warning shots became 300 yd buffers. We still hadn't really seen any combat yet. A couple little harassing fires or a RPG here and there. Mortars and such but I know I myself had not seen any legit combat. So I was pretty fucking nervous.

One morning we all mount up on our tracks and make the push. I will always remember that there was a long long drive just to get off base. We crept past some helos that had their rotors spinning and I could read "dustoff" on the side of the building. I was boot as fuck and asked Rye "what is dustoff?". He explained that they were our medevac birds and I asked "why are they already running?" He looked at me and simply said "they are expecting to get used bro" I had fucking chills run down my spine."

The mission was to get across the Euphrates river to hit a town in the north. The Army was building a pontoon bridge for us to cross. But while approaching the bridge, our convoy was attacked from a town called New Ubaydi. Because of this, we had to push in the city and clear it out otherwise we would have left our flank and rear wide open, which would have been devastating to the Company. As soon as our guys dismounted the tracs to clear the city, we started receiving fire.

"We went out of base and were supposed to be crossing a river on pontoons that the Army (I think) was setting up but they had been taking harassing fire from this little town New Ubaydi. We staged out of town. Not in an offensive posture

at all. I mean we were a click (thousand yards) or so out? I don't even really know. I know we were a ways away but could see helos making gun runs on the town. They called up our snipers and they went up on a hill on what was the near side of town to our position and started taking shots. I figure they were marking targets and shit for air too. I don't know. I was a boot and honestly I was just hoping that whatever was going on in that hornets nest would figure itself out.

Of course it didn't and we made our way to the town. We didn't go directly in though. We sorta skirted it by 500 yds or so and then went in from the far side of town. I was on track security and whoever was up there with me we started hearing shit crack. It took us a second because we really didn't believe we were being shot at. our backs were to the town and all of the sudden it was "oh fuck. this is the real deal," We yelled down to our Marines that this was no joke and then the trackers dropped ramp. The dropped ramp right in this deep ditch so when we got off we basically had an instant trench to fight from but you had to watch it because it was like a 5 foot drop off that ramp.

Rye took a knee up out of the ditch to pack a dip and I yelled at him (even though he was my team leader) to get down. He didn't believe me that it was as hostile as it was until a round struck within 5 inches of his foot. He dropped into the ditch and said "looks like we are popping our cherry today". At one point Rye walked down the middle of the street with his arms in the air yelling "you can't hit me pussies". He told me to look for muzzle flash and engage once I saw it. There were a million windows in that town. I did the best I could firing from the shoulder on the move with a SAW (M249 machine gun).

Our entire squad was supposed to just pull track security when we crossed the river. We didn't really fit in any assault plan and they sure as fuck didn't make a plan for this town. Elliot was our super Jr squad leader so basically 1&2 squads went and then we sorta filled in the center. We had to cross a 4 lane road with rounds pinging off the deck. Sprinting across there I saw Watkins go down on the street I was sprinting to. The first Marine I had actually SEEN get hurt. It was sorta sobering.

Once we entered the town it was house to house. They were staging weapons and then dropping them as they ran to another position with weapons staged. They could move quicker like that and thought we wouldn't shoot an unarmed. We werent even a block in and approached this house on my side of the road. Enemy was on top of the roof but there was no way for me to see them because of the palm trees. The Marines in my squad that went to the roof of the house whos yard I was in didn't even see them. 1st squad was to our left and was radioing that they were smoking people in our lane but we couldnt see them because of all the walls and vegetation. As soon as second squad entered the yard I was covering, all hell broke loose. The enemy on the next roof from my yard opened up with small arms and grenades. Most of second squad came back out of the yard and retreated to the yard they had just came to. I was so fucking confused and still had no idea anything was coming from my side of the road. I turned my SAW towards the front door of the house that they had just been in the yard of. I had the wits about me though to realize not all of them came back out of that yard. As bad as I wanted to put a drum into that door I didn't know where several were. That turned out to be a damn good thing I didnt because Links, Matanick, Dudley, and Bowman were all still in that house. All hit. Leary had lead a one man charge back into the house and had chased the insurgents into the path of a MAAP 50 cal.

We pushed to the next house were they had taken contact from the roof. It was coordinated. It came from inside the house they were entering AND the roof of the house on our side. The house was clear. 1st Squad insisted they shot 2 that were trying to get over a wall. I looked over the roof and one laid there blood gurgling. He was crossing the wall and fell back. We didn't see a second one though."

During all of this our 1st section tracs along with 3/25 1st platoon were pushing down their sector of the town. There were small arms fire everywhere, you could see tracer round deflecting off of buildings and roads. It was chaos. At the end of the day, 1st platoon approached a house that was to be the last house of the day. When they kicked the door in, everything turned bad. LCpl West kicked the door and was immediately shot in both legs. And then Cpl Derga turned to him and was shot in the back. The muj had dug out a basement beneath the first floor and set up a belt fed machine gun with armor piercing rounds. Another machine gun nest was waiting at the top of the stairs aimed at the door. The rest of the squad rushed in, under fire, to get those Marines out of there and secure the building. One of our trackers, Sgt Woullard, got off the trac and rushed in the house as well. While running in a round grazed the side of his face and blew off his kevlar, it spun him around and another shot went through his pack. He fell to the ground but continued to help drag Marines out of the house. The rest of the squad eventually took over the machine gun nests and moved to the second floor to finish clearing the house. That's when SSgt. Goodwin was shot from a gunman hiding in a closet. Eventually we were able to get all Marines out of the house. We pulled back and shot 9 tank rounds into the building to kill the remaining insurgents in there. Afterwards our air dropped a 500 pound bomb on their ass to finish the job. The heroism from 1st Platoon that day was like no other. Marines were rushing in to save their brothers despite the odds, knowing what could possibly be their fate. They kept pushing forward.

Meanwhile back at 3ʳᵈ platoon:

"My Squad Leader and Team Leader decided that they had to go assist 2nd Squad. They turned and looked at me and said "you have the squad" I was like "what the fuck bro??" They insisted I run the squad. I didn't even have fucking comm..

We had an engineer or two with us and they went over to the wall near were the enemy lay dead and set a charge on his RPG he had. It blew and blew out the wall. The other enemy that 1st sqd had shot was on the other side of the wall and as it blew the wall it pushed him into the open. He was waiting for us to enter that yard and shoot at us as his final thing in life. The blast changed his plans.

We had to take the next house. I didn't like going in with a scaled down squad but we had a team of Snipers with us and Sgt Ohara was a badass. He looked at me and said "its your squad Hillberg. You can do this. I am right here." I knew that 1st Squad was to our left but wanted to prep the building. I was afraid of over penetration of the 50 so I had the tracker fire his Mk19 into it. He fired a few rounds and we went in. No resistance at all which is probably good since I was sorta getting my legs under me. This had to have been pretty much concurrent with Rye and Elliot leaving because as he was shooting the Mk19 they were loading up wounded in the back of the track.

We only took like 2 or 3 more buildings that day. 1st Platoon had been hit bad and we all halted in place. We were out of water and I had the worst fucking headache I've ever had.

The trackers had water but had bugged out by this point. We missed our trackers.

Later we all convened at a school. The entire company and we started hearing about all the casualties 1st platoon had taken. Nyen and I got put on roof watch first shift. We were looking down this alley that was so dark but had a couple lights that made it to where our NVGs wouldn't work until they were right on us. Delgado came around and said "WHEN they come tonight. They will come this way. That is why you two are here and not other Marines." Nyen said a prayer and said we'd be alright. They didn't come that night. After watch I went down and laid on the floor. Ohara came and tapped me. He said he had piled bodies that day. Thanked me for letting him go and commended me for how I handled the day."

The next day our guys eventually made it to the pontoon bridge and crossed over. Not far from that we came up on another target town. At first going through the city was normal. Civilians were out and kids were playing. Which is a good sign. But a couple days later the scene changed. All of a sudden, nobody was outside. It was quiet, and in an Iraqi city, quiet is bad. One of our trackers said they saw a water hose still left on with nobody around. Everybody knew something was up.

"We fell back into track security mode and the houses were spread out. I pretty much rode on top of a track and had the Hadji kids fetch me packs of smokes and a toothbrush because i didn't pack on in the hasty leaving of the dam. We were riding on top and the track took a left down this road and then stopped abruptly. We were almost to the house we were going to stay in for the night and i remember getting fucking slammed when he stopped. It was like he went straight from full speed ahead to reverse. He just said "your house is over

there." They backed up and we went maybe 300 yds down the orginal road and offloaded our shit.

We were in the back yard and I was getting Ward and Pomer-inke to chase this rooster because they were both dumb as fuck. All of the sudden an enormous explosion shook us. We grabbed our gear, I don't think I even put a blouse back on. Just grabbed my flack, Kevlar, and weapon and sprinted out the front. 1st platoon had hit an IED about 50 yds from where our tracker stopped and threw it in reverse. We had to secure a LZ so we all ran the couple hundred yards down there and set up a 360. This was the first track I saw blow. It was cooking off all the rounds and just burning and burning. I couldn't tell you how long it took dustoff to get there but is seemed like they just kept coming and coming and coming."

Our 1st section trac, Cpl Rishel's trac, got hit, along with 1st platoon grunts. They rolled over an IED that was supposedly six 155mm artillery rounds. As soon as the blast went off, the driver LCpl Bullock took shrapnel in his shoulder and slammed his face into the steering wheel knocking out his teeth. Cpl Rishel and Sgt Woullard ended up getting shrapnel in their legs. I swear Sgt Woullard has a freaking force field around him. LCpl Shudrowitz who was sitting by the radios, was burned badly head to toe with broken bones and shrapnel all over. We lost six Marines from that blast, and the rest on the trac was wounded badly. The whole inside of the trac was on fire with rounds "cooking off." (firing off rounds because they were on fire) There was blood and body parts everywhere inside, with some Marines on fire. Other Marines were rushing in trying to drag our wounded out of the burning amtrac. The flames got so hot it melted the hull of the trac and started collapsing in on itself. SSgt Woullard, along with other Lima guys, were able to pull out some of the Marines. One Ssgt Payne yelled in the trac if anyone else was alive, and Shudrowitz slowly raised his hand. He then was pulled out and is still alive today. One of our Lima guys, Mike

Strahale, was standing in the back of the trac providing security when the blast hit. He was thrown out of the trac, scraping his torso along the top hinge ripping his stomach wide open. He was thrown about 20 meters from the vehicle, and actually got up and started moving back to the trac with his intestines in his hands. He was in such bad shape that he was triaged and put on the med-evac of Marines that wouldn't make it. He is alive and well to this day, and is actually running the traveling memorial "The Eyes Of Freedom", which honors our KIA Lima guys in that deployment. Horrible day to say the least, it was our first major IED attack on us, and they hit us hard.

> "Everyone felt horrible for 1st Platoon. Two platoon Sergeants in 3 days. So many casualties and KIA in 3 days. I am pretty sure they were removed from the battlefield. Im not positive but I'm pretty sure they were."

1st platoon sustained major casualties during that op. All of Lima did. In just four days, 18 of our guys were wounded and 8 KIA. 1st platoon became combat ineffective and had to be sent out reinforcements from home. During that op, we killed over 150 insurgents and detained 40 more. As well as obtaining proof that the enemy was being reinforced from across the Syrian border. We disrupted the enemy supply line for sure, but we also learned a lot as well. Operation Matador became a learning curve for the rest of the deployment, what worked and what did not work. It is actually used now days as a training guide for Marines back at home. A lot of tragedies during that op, but also a lot of heroes. A lot of which were unsung heroes that received little to no credit for the things they did. But it wasn't about credit with us, it was about each other. And we would do ANYTHING for each other. And finally, on May 17th, our Marines left Al Qaim and came back to the Dam, all changed men.

08 May 2005

Cpl. Dustin A. Derga
SSgt. Anthony Goodwin

11 May 2005

LCpl. Wesley G. Davids
Pfc. Christopher R. Dixon
LCpl. Nicholas B. Erdy
LCpl. Jonathan W. Grant
LCpl. Jourdan L. Grez
SSgt. Kendall H. Ivy

DAVIS AND COLE S MORTAR

MAY 16, 2005

A day I call "Davis's and Cole's mortar". A normal day at the dam, we were out on the ramp (the place where we parked our tracs for maintenance) doing our normal work on the vehicles. Our section (3rd) had just gotten back from Hit so it was us and 2nd section tracs at the Dam. It started out as a normal day. We were on the ramp cleaning out our vehicles and getting them back up and ready for ops. No ops were planned for that day so we had the whole day to work on our vehicles. We had all our tracs staged with the back ramps down, and all our ammo and gear piled up outside the vehicles so we could clean them out and fix all the shit that was broken. I remember sitting and bullshitting with everybody, laughing and cutting up like Marines do. And within a matter of seconds, our world changed. We heard three pops from a distance. Now, up to this point getting mortared was an everyday event, sometimes twice a day. So hearing these pops far off was nothing new to us. I just remember saying "damn they're way off today". Well, they weren't impacts, they were the launches. Not 20 seconds later we heard the scream of one flying in. Typically, when you hear the mortar sound it means its already flying over your head, but this one got louder the closer it got. And we only heard it for about a half of a second, which means it was closing in. And next we heard the sound of the loudest cracking boom. You can almost hear the metal on the mortar round cracking apart. The sky instantly filled up with dark smoke and the smell and taste of gun powder was overwhelming. It was a 120mm mortar round (the big ones) that hit 10 yards from us. To put it in perspective, that's roughly 3 times the size of a hand grenade, fucking huge! It threw shrapnel everywhere. I remember thinking as soon as it hit that we just lost half of our platoon. It was literally chaos. All I remember after that was hearing the screams of Bobby Davis. The mortar hit in a spot where most of us was shielded from it, but the shrapnel hit two of our guys. One piece hit Bobby Davis's left arm at the elbow. His arm was hanging by threads. And another piece hit Matt Cole in the back. He immediately collapsed as soon as it hit hiim. Everything was a blur after that. I just remember everyone, literally everyone rushing around to help. It was as if the entire platoon was running around like ants but everyone somehow knew what purpose they had. Donald Bentz, Jesse Dobbins, and Phillip McKnight pulled Bobby D into one of the tracs working on him. Casey Mattox helped Matt into another trac where Cole Gibbens and Gary Pitcovich were to help with him. A second mortar round impacted on the diesel refueling station 100 yards away, and a third one hit literally 10 feet from us. That third one by some miracle was a dud, and just bounced away from us. I say miracle because by that time we were all scrambling around and if it did explode it would have taken out most of us. It did hit some of our ammo cans and caused them to explode, but that shrapnel blew away from us. We were lucky. I remember Sam Baumgartner took off instantly running to get a humvee so he could med evac them to the top of the dam where our medics were. The humvees was right next to the fuel farm where the second mortar hit, which was all on fire. He was able to find one that ran and hauled ass to us. We loaded up Davis and Cole and Bum drove his ass off, without a flack jacket or rifle, outside the wire so he could take them to the top of the dam. All of this happened in a matter of minutes. I remember afterwards, once we loaded them up and things started settling down on the ramp, that's when reality set in. That's when you start to replay everything that happened and start thinking how things could have been different (good and bad). In the moment of chaos, your body just reacts. Its afterwards when your mind starts to wander, is when it gets hard. Those few minutes was one of the scariest moments of my life. Our day went all to shit in a matter of a second. One minute were laughing and joking, the next minute people are trying to save their lives. The sights, the sounds, and the smells will haunt me forever. Even to this day I still hear the mortar coming in, and the sound of Davis yelling. At the end of it all, Davis lost his arm from the elbow down and Cole was paralyzed from the waist down. As bad as it was though, angels had their wings wrapped around us. Words cannot express how proud of my platoon I was that day. Everyone pulled together and we did what had to be done. If not for those that I mentioned and many more, who knows how different this story could have been. They are my heroes. 3rd Platoon, "Outkast", warriors of Haditha Dam, we are men among men. We are warriors. We are Marines. And I am so proud of all of you! Special acknowledgement to Davis and Cole. I cannot even imagine the road you have had. Just know that we love you and you inspire us daily to be better men. Semper Fi killers.

Jason Teed

311 S IED

The day started out like any other day. We were out on the ramp working on our vehicles when we were briefed on our next op scheduled for that afternoon. My section (3rd section) was supposed to load up a few Marines and do a raid on a house just outside of Haditha. And since our grunts were up north in Operation Matador, we had to find some extra Marines at the dam to help carry out the op. Once we finished getting our vehicles ready, we headed up to the room to get some rest before rolling out. All I could think about in the room is this didn't feel right. Something about this op wasn't settling right with me. So much, that when it was time to head back down to the vehicles I remember looking up at a cross that we had hanging over the room doorway, and I remember saying to myself "come on God, lets go get it done."

We staged our vehicles and loaded up our makeshift grunt team. The time came to go and we rolled out with three tracs, my trac, 311, being last in the convoy. We started heading south on River Road headed for Haditha. A couple miles from the dam there was this monument type structure along with a pedestrian overpass. River Road ran right underneath the overpass and because of the monument there, it was easy to see for miles away. As we approached the overpass, I got this weird feeling once again. Only this time it was stronger. Not two seconds later as we were going underneath the overpass an IED exploded on my vehicle. I remember seeing the actual blast, it felt like someone punched me right in the face. My head blew back and hit the turret hatch, and I blacked out. Next thing I remember is waking up from down in the bottom of the turret looking up out of the hatch. It was dark. All I could see is dirt, smoke, and just shit everywhere. You could taste the asphalt and concrete in the air along with the overwhelming smell of spent explosives. And anybody whos been hit close enough knows that smell all too well and is permanently embedded in your brain. The first thing I did was radio to my section "one one is hit, one one is hit". And as I was trying to climb back up in the turret I called my driver Justin Adams on the radio. "Adams you ok? Adams?" When I got no answer from him I was scared to death to see what happened, I thought for sure he was gone.. I finally made it to the top of the vehicle and saw my crew, still alive!! Milioto who was riding in the seat behind the driver was thrown out of his seat and landed on top of the trac. His face was all bloody because he had busted his nose. Then I saw Adams who was driving was looking around for his comm helmet because it had flown off from the blast, which is why he wasn't answering up. He had a dazed look on his face and there was blood all over him. I then looked back to check my rear crewman Williams. The vehicle was completely covered with dirt and pieces of the road. The debris was still falling on us like snow. And through all that Williams reached up and gave me a thumbs up that they were all good. I remember the first thing I did was thank God that everyone was still alive. Then all I could think about was we needed to get the hell out of there in case of a second attack. A common tactic for those goat fuckers is to hit you with an IED to stop you and then ambush or drive a suicide car bomb into you. So I looked at Adams and said "Push forward, push forward. Go Go, Get us out of the kill zone". Adams fired the beast back up and we rolled right out of the IED crater. Once we pushed through we repositioned the vehicle and opened fire on the trigger man that was in a nearby shack. We let the grunts out and continued on with the original op. We kept pushing forward.

The whole incident probably lasted about a minute. But like Adams said everything was in slow motion. All up until it was time to push through the kill zone, then reality set in and time started to speed up again. The actual IED was one 155mm artillery round and possibly a mine. The blast was big enough to completely stop a 30 ton amtrac moving about 25 mph. The crater it left was ten feet wide and four feet deep. The IED popped just underneath the front of the vehicle. Half a second sooner and surely all the shrapnel would have taken our heads off, and half a second later the blast would have been right underneath our feet. We had shrapnel the size of coke cans and notebooks stuck all in the front of the trac. The whole front end had a huge bow in it and it actually pushed the engine inside back about an inch. There was pieces of the road covering the top of the vehicle and all in the back. The boom was big enough that people inside the dam two miles away felt it. Adams ended up with a busted lip. Milioto busted his nose and blew one of his eardrums. I had a busted knee and back issues from when I fell and few scratches on my face probably from rocks or debris in the blast. God was definitely with us that day. Of all the fucked up days we had over there, that one I consider one of the good ones because we all made it through. But even so, from that point on our lives changed.

OPERATION NEW MARKET

MAY 23-29

This operation was solely based on Haditha. One of our foot patrols was contacted by small arms fire outside of the city of Haditha just days before the operation. So our main objective was to go back there and put an end to the enemy growth that was developing in the city.

It started on May 23rd, we drove our tracks up to Haditha and let our grunts out to do what they do. Several minutes after they were inserted, we started receiving enemy fire once again. During that fire fight we lost one Marine and another one wounded. The fight didn't last very long though, maybe 20 minutes. But it was enough evidence to determine that the Muj had developed a small stronghold in Haditha. We ended up killing dozens of insurgents and several others wounded. For a few days that alone stopped enemy attacks. We had started pushing them further and further on the run. We had that the number one leader of insurgents, Al Zarqawi, was in the city conducting attacks. So when we arrived at the city, we were on the hunt.

Several days went by, just the normal clearing houses and capturing weapons caches. We drove up to an elementary school to setup a small FOB. I remember pulling up to the school, and setting in place to secure the outer perimeter. Not five minutes after arriving we started getting mortared. One round literally landed five feet from my vehicle. But luckily our trac dug up enough sand by turning into our position that the round sunk into the soft sand and detonated. We heard another one come flying in, but it must have been a dud because it never exploded. Once again, another close call. I brought the mortar fin inside the school to turn in to the COC. Inside there I saw all kinds of insurgent propaganda displayed all over the walls. "Do not trust the Crusaders, do not be caught talking to the Crusaders." In other words, they were threatening even the KIDS not to talk to us. Trying to poison their minds like all insurgents do.

The very next day my buddy Cpl Perry's track hit a double stack mine in a small FOB further in the city. We were all getting ready to leave the city when he got hit. Luckily none of our infantry was on the vehicle. No casualties happened. The double stack destroyed several road wheels on the track, and severely hit the deck plates and radios. We had already started sand bagging the deck of the vehicles to hopefully absorb any blasts like that. Apparently, it worked. None of my brothers were wounded in the blast.

Overall, two amtracs were hit with land mines, and two other Humvees were hit with IEDs. We had one KIA and one wounded during the whole operation. Another fun fact, is that supposedly during one of the fire fights, we shot and wounded Al Zarqawi. Which was a HUGE win for us. The operation was only supposed to last two days, but after the engagements it lasted about six days. All in all it was a very successful op. We killed several insurgents, wounded many, detained many, blew up several weapons caches, and wounded the number one insurgent in Iraq. Which was probably the reason the insurgents were trying to fight us there. Not many times do you consider an operation where we lost Marines a successful one, but this solidified our presence there and we left a major statement to them, We're Coming For You.

5-25-05
Sgt David N. Winburg
5-26-05
Maj. Ricardo A. Crocker

HUMVEE ON GRIZZLIES

09 JUNE 2005

June 9th. Just another day operation. Our 1st section tracs, 1st platoon grunts, and tanks, went out for a small op to raid a house. There's no easy way to tell this story than to just lead right into it. Our guys were heading out to Haqlaniyah to do the op. They drove down South Dam Rd and turned left on Grizzlies Rd heading toward the city with tanks in the lead. The lead tank pushed up ahead a little bit and turned on Texas Trail Rd to secure the path for our convoy to move. Just then they hit a massive IED. It was three 155mm rounds and several more explosives with it. It was enough to fuck the tank up, killing one of our tankers and injuring 3. After the explosion, Weapons Co came up to med-evac the Marines. They loaded up the KIA and wounded on several Humvees and headed back towards the dam. About a couple hundred meters from the tanks IED, one of the Humvees hit another IED. This time the IED killed four more Marines. One more tanker and three Weapons Co. It was a horrible horrible event. That one tanker survived one blast just to be killed in another minutes later. It was as if the muj planned the whole event. My buddy Stephan Arnold loaded up the KIA on his trac. He said one of the guys was just a torso. I remember other people saying while waiting on the forensics team to show up, they had to shoot dogs from trying to eat the body parts that were still laid out in the area. A dark day for us for sure.

"It makes you wonder how there can be a God in events like that day. Such a horrible event. No man should ever see anything like that, but sadly that was a normal day in Iraq 2005". (from my journal) My heart aches and bleeds everyday just thinking about that day and those Marines and their families. How the hell do you explain days like that to people. Just when you think things cant get any more fucked, just when you think you've seen the worst that there is, days like this happens. I truly believe this is about the point where the numbness started setting in. Its like shit just kept piling on top of shit, and the more it happened the more we became like zombies. Those 30 minutes put a hole in our hearts for the rest of our lives. Days like that make it hard to believe in our cause over there. But we kept believing, we kept pushing forward. Even though it was hard, we kept pushing forward.

09 June 2005

LCpl. Dustin V. Birch
LCpl. Daniel Chavez
LCpl. Thomas O. Keeling
LCpl. Devon P. Seymour
Cpl. Brad D. Squires

OPERATION SPEAR

JUNE 17-20

O nce again we went back up north to the Syrian border. This time in the city of Karabilah. along with 3/2. Our objective was to once again destroy the stronghold coming through Syria. This was going to be a quick operation right before Operation Sword in the city Hit. Once again we were met with more resistance. Now, I wasn't there for this operation, but this portion of the book and our deployment needs to be shared. We learned a lot of lessons from Operation Matador. So the whole outlook on this operation was very different. We weren't going to roll through this city by being polite. We were going to do what Marines do. We come like Devil Dogs, we put the fear of God in them, and we destroy them. That's the fight we know how to fight, what we were trained to fight.

Coming into Karabilah was a different mindset. We didn't want another Matador on our hands. So in response to the insurgents, we wanted to make a statement that we weren't letting the insurgents come into the country and take over. They would need to come through us first. And that's the game we played. Clearing the city was none like any other. We started using more of our assets during this op. One of which was with one of our Amtracs, called a MICLIC. Basically a C4 line charge that can be shot out of an Amtrac and blow up everything in its path. (picture throwing a rope as far as you can and the entire

74

rope flies in a long line, except the entire line is full of C4 and all of it detonates). That's what we started using to clear the roads. We knew that anyone in the city at this point knew what was coming, and the ones that remained when we came, we knew they weren't friendly. The streets and houses was cleared with C4, Amtrac 50cal, 240 golfs, 249 saws, and the brute strength of our GRUNTS that kicked in doors and took names. We weren't taking shit from anything that looked suspicious. That was the mindset at this point. We had to make a statement to the ones trying to flood through from Syria, but to let the insurgents further south know that we weren't fucking around. And we most definitely made that statement. Literally every path/road/alley that we passed through came to a complete destruction. Not that we were trying to destroy the city, but making a statement: "Don't Resist"

We came out of that with no wounded and no KIA. We killed scores of insurgents, destroyed several IED making factories, and over 30 cars ready for suicide bombing. We did many things through that operation. Learned many things also. Send in Marines let them do what they do, we will prevail and conquer.

"Overall it was the most kinetic operation I was on. It seemed like everyday once it started had a lot going on. Casualties were low compared to Matador, but it seems like there was a lot of fighting. Maybe it really wasn't that bad, but both at the time and in my memory I thought it was bad."

> *"I remember attacking the city right when the sun came up with all the tracs on line and Cobras above us. The grunts got off right at the edge of the city and we started clearing from there."*

> *'The funniest thing I remember is that SSgt Payne wanted us to stay off the roads as much as possible, or at least ones that hadn't been proofed yet. So we drove through a lot of walls and through courthouses instead of taking side roads. A Civil Affairs officer yelled at Payne about it and he told*

him to fuck off. I remember driving through four separate walls of the same compound. It was a lot of fun."

"At one point a tank was directly on the side of my AAV and fired multiple main gun rounds at a house in front of us that we were getting shot from. The MICLIC track from H&S Co fired a line charge down a street. One of the line charges landed on a bunch of houses along the road and blew them all up. Then a tank, SSgt Payne's trac, and my trac drove down that road and it was completely covered with rubble. I forget how many other times they fired MICLICs, but it was a few other times. Just like with Op Matador, we left Haditha at night and drove through the night to get to Karabilah. It was 8-9 hours and a terrible drive."

~Blaine Ballard~

In other words, Marines did what they had to do!

THE OP THAT NEVER HAPPENED

Not much to say really about this, but it drives a good point so I decided to include this in the book. It was a normal day at the dam, we were all out there working on our vehicles. My section (3rd section) received word that we were linking up with our grunts that afternoon for an op in Haditha. We were supposed to do a raid on a house. The plan was for the grunts to helicopter in the city, dismount, and secure the house. While they were doing that we were supposed to drive straight to the house, load up our grunts along with any weapons and detainees, and extract back to the dam. So after they briefed us on it, we went back up to the room to rest up for that afternoon. Now, I can't exactly put into words the feeling I had at that moment but the best I can describe it is something felt off, way off. Deep in the pit of my stomach I just had a bad feeling about this op. Not that we didn't always have a bad feeling about every op we did, but this one was different. Somehow I just knew something bad was going to happen. I tried to blow it off the best I could and rest up but it wouldn't leave my mind. So that afternoon came and it was time to gear up and prep the vehicles. We get everything ready, fire up the vehicles, stage them in line, and waited on the word to roll out. Again, I couldn't shake this feeling. And the longer we waited the feeling steadily got worse. Our platoon sergeant walked by my vehicle, pointed at me, and said "yall be careful". Which is something he has NEVER done before and of course this didn't help my gut feeling either. We probably waited about 30 minutes for the word until finally they

82

came out and told us that the op was cancelled. There was a sandstorm coming in and they didn't want to fly the helos in it. Seriously I can't even begin to explain to you the relief I felt at that moment. And whats crazier is every single person I talked to afterwards said the exact same thing. They all had that same feeling that something was different with this one and something bad was going to happen. Moral of this story, ALWAYS trust your gut. Listen to that little voice inside, that's the good Lord speaking to you.

OPERATION SWORD

27 JUNE 2005 - 21 JULY 2005

For months now we have been told about this Operation. The city of Hit was supposed to be the next Fallujah. Hell, we've been hearing that since Camp Lejeune during our work ups. Really the only thing we heard was that Hit was the strong hold of the insurgents and we were going to go in and clear them fuckers out. The plan of attack was push in from the north and move south through the city, and 3/25 Lima (us) was going to be the main effort. That's about it. So naturally tensions were high for the months leading up to this event. Well finally on June 27th it was our time to make it happen.

We left the dam the day before that and staged out vehicles at Al Asad air base. This is the great and wonderous air base of the Marine Corps where they have ice cream and ice. I remember thinking at least we were gonna get a couple good meals in before this epic battle. The next evening we staged right near the entrance of the base, getting ready to roll out. It was about a 45 minute drive to get to Hit. Just before we pushed out I remember hearing on the radio that Recon hit contact on the outskirts of the city. They were in a pretty heavy firefight. As soon as we heard that the entire convoy pushed out. I remember thinking the whole way there that we were about to get into some heavy shit. That 45 minute drive will play some fucking games with your head anticipating what was about to come. Longest drive of my life it seemed like.

We finally pulled up to the city. Instead of the original plan of pushing down from the north, we entered the city from the south. The rest of the battalion surrounded the city not letting anybody in or out. And 3/25 Lima, Weapons company, our Iraqi ING, and one Army platoon came in from the south and started pushing north. This was the first time in Iraq history that a weaponized Iraqi platoon combined up with US Marines to capture enemy territory. We (3/25 Lima) were the lead element approaching the city. The first few vehicles entered in and I remember all of a sudden I heard 3 loud ass explosions. The first two were IED's set up for us for when we entered. One popped behind my vehicle, but none of the blasts hit anyone. The 3rd blast was one of our tanks popping a tank round into a shack nearby, where the trigger man was hiding out. 120mm tank round vs a goat fucker, guess which one prevailed. Those three booms shook us pretty good because at that point we knew we were in some shit. Instantly we dismounted our grunts and started Operation Sword.

Within a few hours we cleared a good portion of the city. After the first few minutes of entering we figured it would be chaos, but actually it went fairly smoothly. We finally had some day light and was pushing through pretty quickly, with no issues. We were all lined up east to west, sectioned off facing north on every road, and pushing simultaneously clearing every house, every corner, every alley. Tanks were pushed ahead of us moving up and down the roads checking for IED's and any enemy threats. During the first few hours of the operation we really didn't find any insurgents, but what we did find was a ton of weapons caches. It was at this point we realized that all this talk about us entering from the north, somehow we knew that the insurgents would get this intel at some point. So they were ready to fight us on the north side, and their weapons caches were in the south for them to fall back and resupply. We apparently outsmarted the fuck out of them on this one. And actually for the next few days it was a fairly smooth operation. The infrastructure of the city was in ruins, including a mosque that was blown up and damn near crumbling down. All done by the fucking insurgents, to try to put fear into the civilians of the city. We encountered a few detainees and more weapons caches. But not one ounce of resistance. We just knew that the further north we would get the more resistance we would have. But after a couple days of clearing the more optimistic we became. Really at first, the only downside to the op was the fucking heat. It was absolutely stupid. Temperatures were getting over 120 degrees, so being out there in our flack jackets and kevlar helmets it was borderline unbearable. It was the hottest time of the year during that op, and we were sitting in our big metal amtracs cooking. It was so hot in fact, you could put your MRE meal on top of the trac and it would cook in a few minutes. A good hot meal and boiling water, what's not to love about that. I swear I lost 10 pounds on that op alone.

I remember after the second day of clearing, we set up for the night. There's something extremely eerie about being in an Iraqi city in the middle of the night, I really can't explain it. At night, at least on the vehicle, you're the only one awake guarding your post. It's just you in the turret, standing between your guys and the enemy. You're up, staring at the dark green image through your night vision, waiting for the worst to happen. You hear every little noise, every bark from a dog, every piece of garbage that blows in the wind. And every sound you hear you think the worst of it. It's creepy as hell. Long nights inside the city, you really find out who you are and what you're made of. I remember standing watch that night just thinking that something is eventually is going to turn to shit, we just have to be ready.

The next day we push further north through the city. We eventually got past a main highway that ran east/west on the northern sector of the city. After this point it was sort of their version of the ghetto. That's where we expected to see resistance. As soon as we pushed north of that road I remember smelling marijuana in the air. Which is a bad sign when you're clearing a city. We knew they were there, but we couldn't do anything unless they fired first. We ended up reaching the north end of the city, we cleared the entire city with no resistance. After we reached the end, we discovered that the road leading into the city from the north end was wired with IEDs. About a mile length of IEDs daisy chained so that it would all detonate at the same time. They were planning on us entering in from the north and set it up to blow up the convoy coming in. So we knew that they were there amongst us, ready to fight. But with our rules of engagement, we couldn't do anything unless we were attacked first. Our hands were tied.

After clearing the city we set up two Firm Bases. (fortified bases within the city where we can operate in and out of). Firm Base 1 was further south in the city, and Firm Base 2 was further north off that main highway. We had just spent 4 days clearing the city, but that wasn't over for us. We knew they were still there in the city, so we decided to op daily within the city to draw them out. Our 4 day op turned into about a month. I was at Firm Base 2, which was an old hotel that we took over. We patrolled daily around the city looking for anything suspicious. After a few days we encountered our first attack. Firm Base 1 took an SVBIED. The SUV drove straight into their firm base and detonated, followed by small arms fire. The attack killed two of Kilo Co. Marines and wounded several more. We knew then that they were ready to come out and play. Later that night we were mortared at Firm Base 2. Three rounds landed close to us but not on top of us. We sent a patrol out to where the rounds were fired from but Im not sure whatever happened with that. We would get random pop shots here and there, one time in particular I remember an RPG flying over our heads. But they just would not stand up to us toe to toe. We had a few IEDs go off amongst us, one in particular hit the vehicle of my crewman Adams's younger brother who was out there. We responded to the scene and towed the Amtrac back. It was a large IED off the main east west highway. A few burn and shrapnel injuries but all survived, luckily. At some point while we were there, our Weapons company stopped a major mortar attack. Some how across the river they were driving in their 5 ton truck, which sat up high in the air. They just peeped over a sand hill and saw several muj with multiple mortar tubes getting ready to mortar the shit out of both firm bases. Needless to say they ended that real fast, and apparently this wasn't just some random dumb muj attack. This was their professional mortar squad. If not for those Weapons guys, I might not be here today writing this shit.

July 15th. We had a foot patrol out of Firm Base 2, our grunts along with some of the ING. During the foot patrol our guys passed in front of a mosque. Along the wall of the mosque an IED detonated through the wall into the street where we were walking. One of our guys went down instantly, Doc Youngblood. Since our fucked up rules of engagement prevented us from going in the mosque to clear it out, we sent in our Iraqi squad. They went in like dogs from hell and pulled out the trigger man. We all came back to Firm Base 2 with the trigger man, and the Iraqis proceeded to beat the ever living shit out of him. It was a beautiful sight. I remember watching this beating thinking about how frustrated those ING guys must have been. They're out here giving their all to take their country back and these insurgent cocksuckers keep fucking things up. I honestly don't know how they didn't kill the muj mother fucker. We just sat back and let them beat the shit out of him. I really feel like they needed to get that out of their system. It's like I was watching history in the making right there. Good guys versus bad guys, good versus evil, patriots versus cocksuckers. It was the early stages of Iraq standing on their own two feet.

After about a month or so we left that city, we had some Marines do a relief in place with us. The plan was to maintain security in that city so that insurgents wouldn't overtake it any more. We did our job and set up a secure and stable city. All and all despite our losses it was a successful operation. We flushed our most of the muj that was in there, we crushed all their weapons caches, and setup security so that they could not regain a stronghold in that city. We also set up the city to where they could repair their infrastructure, including the crumbling mosque. During the operation we lost three Marines. Two on July 10th during the SVBIED attack, and Doc Youngblood several days later from the injuries during the July 15 attack. Our hearts were broken from those three Marines. But despite that, we successfully cleared the city with no major engagements. We outsmarted them and crushed their stronghold. We fucked up their moral. We did it right there.

10 July 2005

SSgt. Joseph P. Goodrich
LCpl. Ryan J. Kovacicek

21 July 2005

HM3 Travis L. Youngboood

OPERATION SABRE

28 JULY 2005 – 31 JULY 2005

Operation Sabre was a last minute planned operation. The city was Cykla, a small fisher town directly north of the Dam. As far as I can remember, the reason we decided to go there was because of intel of insurgency going on there. Also we wanted to show our presence to the locals in that area since it was so close to the Dam. This op was planned and conducted just days after we returned home from Hit. We really didn't expect to see much activity there, but that all changed on July 28. The plan was to send one section of our tracs (2nd section), all of Lima grunts along with our Iraqi ING, and tanks. We set out for Cykla the morning of the 28th. Once getting there it was the normal searching of the houses. Since we weren't technically trying to clear the city it was more of a casual knocking on the doors and talking to the people with the presence of force. Everything started out fine but not long after we got there we started taking fire.

Once again, I was not there for this op. A close brother of mine and true warrior Cole Gibbens will give his experience. His experience word for word is italicized. This is the story of Cylka, Iraq.

"I remember it like yesterday. Cykla was a small fishing town visible on the distant horizon from the Dam. We had been running hard for the past few months and everyone including

the grunts were worn out. This op was kind of thrown on us last minute and we weren't too excited about going on it. We all sat down the previous evening after Otter (SSgt Scott Ottesen) had gotten back from the brief and were given our orders and designated duties. I was designated medivac and was pretty pissed that I had to sit this one out on the sidelines. Watching my brothers go into battle was never easy but little did I know this little fishing town was about to give us a punch right in the mouth."

"We rolled at daybreak the next morning and made the 2 hr drive to the town. Cordon and Knock was our mission to make our presence felt, and look for some punk ass muslims hiding in this town to see if they had any weapons. We pulled into the town like Marines do which pretty much means (like you own the fucker). The other tracks in my section along with the grunts from my track rolled into town and started their mission. Me, Otter, and Eury stayed back and waited."

"The mission started out quiet and it was a hot mother that day. Being that we were medivac we kept the track running and were chit chatting and what not, listening to what was coming over comms, when all hell broke loose. We could hear the gunfire over the engine and knew that the boys had gotten into a pretty good gunfight. I remember hearing the call we need a medivac and were given the coordinates. Little did I know what we were going into, but nothing would have stopped me from helping my brothers, I started into the village before grid was even finished."

After a few houses of talking with the locals, we approached a house that was full of insurgents. Immediately after knocking, we started taking fire from that house. Cpl Williams was immediately shot from inside through the door. Several of our Marines were hit including an

Iraqi ING, but we were still able to pull back and return fire on them. There were four insurgents in that building. They were doped up on adrenaline and other drugs giving them an extreme tolerance. They fled that house and ran into another house that was under construction. Two of the insurgents were killed running but the other two made it to the house. Instead of rushing in right away after the insurgents, we decided to put five tank rounds and a few thousand M16 rounds into the building first. That's when LCpl Lyons squad went in to access the dead and kill the remaining. The insurgents were so amped up on drugs that even after all of that, they were still firing back. As soon as LCpl Lyons entered, he was hit. That's when Gibbens was called out to med-evac our wounded. He rushed into the city to get to our Marines as fast as he could. Once there, and under fire, he was able to load up the Marines and evac them out of the city. The firefight soon turned into a massive ammo dump on this house. We were able to surround the insurgents and keep suppressive fire on them keeping them pinned down.

"I was blazing into town to get my boys, Otter was on point giving me directions on the fly. We arrived at the location, but they were still pinned down. They asked for cover from the track which was obliged. The original call said 1 marine wounded and 3 KIA, still not knowing who they were. I was being waved at by a marine off to my right whom I could see needed help and then he started taking fire. So I re-positioned the vehicle in the line of fire and dismounted from the vehicle without my weapon while telling Eury to open the back hatch. I sprinted over and grabbed the first Marine I could while the other grunts who weren't pinned down provided cover and assisted with the carrying of the 2 others. This all seems like it was in slow motion and took forever but when the juice is pumping you really have no idea. We got them loaded in the back and snagged the DOC who joined us as well. I remember looking up at Otter and seeing the hand *wave saying get back to the trac. As I was climbing back up, we started taking fire again from the left and was hitting all over the track. I dove in head first and got that bad boy outta there and back to the chopper awaiting us."*

As soon as they left the sight, the rest of Lima surrounded the house and unloaded on those fuckers. Surrounding the house we could see if the insurgents would attempt to escape, so we kept shooting to pin them down and keep them isolated. Eventually we killed the third insurgent and spotted the remaining insurgent still crawling reaching for his weapon. After several magazines of 5.56 ammo into this guy, he finally bleed out. And to put the cherry on top, our air support ended up dropping a 500 pound bomb on their ass. We actually have video of that fucker flying up and falling down from that blast.

"Once back at the rendezvous, we were able to drop our guards and lend assistance to the medic. When I got to the back of the trac and realized who it was, I was floored. Lyons my grunt radio operator was lying there motionless, along with Williams. There was nothing we could do. We did what we could, but our brothers had already gone home."

Despite our wounded and losses, it was a perfectly executed counter attack on the insurgents. Our boys fought well that day. During that op we lost two of our Marines, Cpl Williams and LCpl Lyons, and one Iraqi ING. Even though we kicked their ass, it will still never replace our brothers. They fought hard, they fought like warriors, and gave their lives defending us.

28 July 2005

LCpl. Christopher P. Lyons
Cpl. Andre L. Williams

OPERATION QUICK STRIKE

01 AUGUST 2005 – 09 AUGUST 2005

I have been dreading writing this chapter since the day I started this book. In fact, I've dreaded it so much that I put it off to one of the very last chapters I've written. To tell the story of Operation Quick Strike I have to put myself into a deep dark place that ive avoided for so many years. I honestly don't know how to tell this story. It was by far the worst time of my life, and the same for so many others that was there. No words can explain the pain that goes through us when even thinking about this, let alone trying to put this into words. I only hope that I can honor these warriors the way that they should be honored. Operation Quick Strike, the operation from Hell, the operation that changed the course of the Iraq war, this is our story.....

The city of Barwanah had been on our radar for several weeks now. We already cleared it once before, but like many other cities as soon as we leave, the insurgents flood back in and reorganize. We knew of some shady activity going on in Barwanah, so before we planned a full out operation we decided to insert two teams of snipers to overwatch and gather intell. So sometime in late July that's what we did. Six snipers were inserted just on the outside of Barwanah. Back at the Dam we had just finished up Cykla and was regrouping from that op. On August 1st we got word that our snipers had been attacked and we all needed to head out. At first we didn't really get the full story, but we scrambled our asses off to gear up for the QRF. Our two teams of snipers were all on overwatch in the middle of the day when they were all of a sudden ambushed. They're position was compromised, and they started receiving mortar fire. Mortars were raining down on them and immediately after the rounds hit a squad of insurgents rushed in on them. They attacked with AKs and RPGs. Our snipers fought back but eventually were overrun. Initially they killed five of our Marines with one Marine badly wounded. Those mother fuckers captured our wounded brother and drug his body off through the streets of Barwanah. When we arrived there, we discovered that they had captured one of our guys. At that point, some of our grunts loaded up on aluminum boats to patrol up and down the river searching for any sign of the missing Marine. They soon hit contact (firefight) on the banks of Barwanah and Haditha and did gun runs up and down the river, but found no trace of the body. That is what started Operation Quick Strike. Our primary objective was to push into Barwanah and recover the Marine that they had taken as well as flush out the insurgents there. Within a day a Battalion size operation was planned and assembled. On the evening of August 2nd, we were all staged outside of the city waiting on the word to move out. I remember going over to my buddy Stewart's trac to bullshit with him. I remember me, him, and Waruinge were laughing about something to do with energy drinks, I don't fully remember what it was we were laughing about, but ill never forget that moment. That was the last time I saw my buddies. On the morning of August 3rd, we started to push towards the city of Barwanah.

The morning of August 3rd was sort of a strange one. We were up getting things ready before dawn like we usually do. But there was a change in the order of march into the city, also a few personnel changes on the vehicles. Ill get into more of that later, but once we got our orders we started to push out. It was a straight shot to the city. We had a lot of the Iraqi National Guard with us too, which all rode in they're little civilian trucks we called Tonka trucks. Because of that, we had to take paved roads to get to the city, those Tonka trucks couldn't go offroad the way we could. Our LAR vehicles and tanks pushed out in front followed by our tracs. LAR was the first to approach the city and set up road watch while we pushed closer in. For all intents and purposes, the roads seemed clear for us to drive on. So we were cleared to begin the operation. During the changes of order, my vehicle was pushed towards the end of the convoy. Ill never forget as we got closer in, I saw the largest explosion I have ever seen in my life. I swear the flame towered up a couple hundred feet and the concussion took your breath away. It was so large my first thought once seeing it was the small refinery/storage tanks directly south of the city had blown up. It wasn't until the radio call that "a very large IED had exploded" that I realized it was one of us. When the Amtracs approached the city, the first two vehicles turned right to enter the city. As the third trac was about to turn, the IED went off. It was triggered by someone nearby, they used det-cord to ignite the blast. The IED consisted of ten 155mm artillery rounds and a 6ft propane tank on top. They actually dug up the asphalt, placed a 1" thick metal plate down so that the blast would go straight up, placed the munitions down, then re-asphalted the road. There was literally no way we could have even noticed that something was there. The blast hit on the tail end of the trac, and flipped over the 27 ton vehicle upside down and 30 meters ahead. The back end of the vehicle split wide open. Never have I seen so much carnage from a vehicle. There were parts of the trac and parts of our Marines spread out over a 50 meter radius. Worst thing I have ever seen. For all of us, everything after that became numb. As soon as the blast went off, the first two tracs unloaded the infantry and started clearing the nearby houses. We secured the general area and setup a perimeter so we could regroup. The rest of the vehicles came to a halt, for fear there were more IEDs on the road. Ill never forget when I heard who's vehicle it was. SSgt Payne came over the radio and said the names – Stewart, Wariunge, Harper, and Borne. My heart just sank. I was in utter disbelief. The hard part was we couldn't even react to it, we couldn't even break down and let it out. We were all still on watch securing our sectors. It was as if we had to bury it deep and keep on pushing. The worst thing we have ever seen and we couldn't even shed a tear. We still had a job to do. On that amtrac was 3/25 3rd Platoon

1ˢᵗ squad. In an instant, we just lost 14 Marines and one interpreter. In one of the secured buildings, the rest of 3/25 3ʳᵈ platoon was setup. Since they just lost a third of their platoon, they were given the option to pull out and head back to the Dam to mourn their brothers. One of the grunts said "fuck that, they didn't bitch out on Iwo Jima we aint about to bitch out now." And they all agreed to finish out the operation. That's balls on a whole new level. I have so much respect for those hard mother fuckers, 3/25 Lima Co are legends, hands down! The rest of the platoon went out to attempt to recover the bodies and equipment, and try to positive identify the Marines who were killed. All that was left of some of the Marines were the name tag from their cammies. It was a horrific scene, unfortunately most of the Marines weren't able to be positively identified, no way possible.

There was one Marine that was on that squad but wasn't on that vehicle that day. That morning when the march order changed, Travis Williams was pulled from that trac and moved to another vehicle just minutes before stepping off. As hard as that one move was on him, dealing with the guilt all these years later, he was saved that day. God had different plans for him. Also one thing that's not commonly talked about in the reports is that one Marine in fact survived the blast. Chris Borne from our trac platoon. He was the driver. The blast was so powerful that the Marine sitting a few feet behind him was completely gone. And by sheer miracle Borne literally crawled away from the trac after it had flipped. After the blast the rounds from inside the vehicle was "cooking off". One of the LAR vehicles actually drove in between Borne and the trac to protect him from the rounds so he could be recovered. Again, that's heroism on a different level. Shielding your brother by putting yourself in the way. Borne was soon med-evac'd and to this day is still alive. Angels were covering him with their wings that day.

After the chaos, we continued to push into the city, clearing anything and everything. Every house, every room, every alley, every ditch. We searched everywhere for those fuckers. We had a few engagements during the op. Most were firing from across the river in Haditha. One of our tanks took an RPG, but they quickly returned fire and eliminated the threat. Our Iraqi force that was with us was fucking the muj up too. Any sound they would hear down an alley they would open fire. We pushed the insurgents all the way through the city until they had no choice but to fight back or jump into the Euphrates river. And once they jumped in we had F-18s doing gun runs, lighting those mother fuckers up. We had 500 pound bombs dropped on the house across the river we were taking fire from. We unloaded the fury.

A couple days into the op we got word that our Sniper's body had been recovered. Apparently, he died that day of the attack and the muj drug his body across the river into Haditha and left him in the street. Obliviously it was a setup trying to pull us in so they could ambush us. But during the night a special ops Delta Force team went in the city and recovered the Marine. How they accomplished that, that's another story. But those bad mother fuckers did it! No man left behind.

The op lasted about a week. After the operation was over we loaded up and headed back to the Dam. I remember that day vividly. It was the most scared I have ever been. We took asphalt roads the whole way back. I just knew that we were gonna get popped again since the enemy had a solid week to plan an attack for us. I was shaking the entire ride back. Some of our guys were throwing up in the back of the amtracs. It was a long fucked up ride back. We found a few mines and IEDs on the way, but we eliminated them and made it back to the Dam safely.

That operation changed everything. After the operation the entire Marine Corps changed their tactics. From that day forward the Marine Corps no longer used Amtracs in Iraq to transport our infantry. Tracs were obviously the main target, so aftwards we used 5 ton trucks and eventually had MRAP vehicles because they could take IEDs better. Unfortunately it took losing so many of our guys to get to that point. Operation Quick Strike was the last major operation we did in our deployment. We did more than our share, and it was time for us to get a break.

Over all we killed roughly 40 of those mother fuckers. But even still it will never compare to the ones we lost that day. After that op we all felt like our time was coming, it was just a matter of when. We all lost a huge part of us in Iraq, and I believe most of that part was in Barwanah. We had just lost 20 Marines in a three day span. We left that city about 6 days later, all changed men. But what little we had left, our boys kept pushing forward, we kept fighting. We completed the mission and completed the deployment. But that operation remains in all of us to this day, every single day.

01 August 2005
Cpl. Jeffrey A. Boskovitch
Lcpl. Roger D. Castleberry Jr.
Sgt. David J. Coullard
Lcpl. Daniel N. Deyarmin Jr.
Lcpl. Brian P. Montgomery
Sgt. Nathaniel S. Rock

03 August 2005
Cpl David Stewart
Lcpl Kevin Waruinge
Sgt Bradley Harper
Sgt Justin Hoffman
Lcpl Timothy Bell Jr
Lcpl Eric Bernholtz
Lcpl Michael Cifuentes
Lcpl Christopher Dyer
Sgt David Kreuter
Lcpl Aaron Reed
Lcpl William Wightman
Lcpl Edward Schroeder II
Lcpl Nicholas Bloem
Lcpl Grant Fraser

RETROGRADE

After the events of Operation Quick Strike, we carried out a few operations until our relief came. We were so relieved to see our replacements, knowing that we were going home. We did the best we could to show them how the enemy was and how they're willing to fight. But deep down, we were ready to leave that world behind. We went home, with little to no debriefing about the things we saw. We were literally in country fighting the muj mother fuckers one day, then loading up to go home the next. We left the battlefield one day, and was back in the states the next. No debriefing afterwards. We were literally put back into society days after that deployment. I remember in North Carolina going to the movies and heard a car backfire on the street. Nearly had my heart racing and looking for cover. In those times, there was no transition back into the real world. We were on our own. To this day, there still is little help to get our lives back on track. It's a switch that were trained to turn on, but no direction to turn it back off. I guess once they're finished with us, its like "good luck fuckers", and send us on our way. Typical VA I guess. We're just a number, not an individual. We had to learn our path afterwards on our own. Not saying that were not elite enough to do so, and many of us did. But we were thrown to the wolves afterwards. In our world, Marines fight their way through. Which is what we try to do still. But that's not how America works. We get rejected for so many things right off the bat because we're "war torn". Unfortunately the very people that defend our very freedom, have the hardest road to success. In many times result in suicide. Here now many years later, I have had 6 of my platoon brothers commit suicide because they couldn't cope with the world thrown at them. Which is the case of MANY combat veterans. We're dropped back off in a world that we no longer recognize and are told to deal with it. Its an unfair expectation for us to do that. We were once jolly green giants walking the earth, but back home, were just a spec in most peoples lives. And most of those people were at the mall the whole time. We're up against the impossible at times. Which is just one reason that im writing this book. Of all the struggles we go through, survivors guilt, our memories, what we had to do to survive, where does that make sense in todays world. We gave our ALL, and we aren't even recognized. Im not asking for sympathy from anyone, I signed up to do what I asked, just like all of us. But where is our recognition? Where is our support? What more can we give to our beloved country, the United States Of America, to appreciate what the cost is?

LIFE AFTER COMBAT

October, 2018

Its been 13 years since we stepped off the battlefield. 13 years, and it still seems like yesterday. I can still see it, still hear it, still smell it, still taste it. Everyday something triggers me and instantly im back in Iraq. We all experienced something different over there, and we all accept and cope with it in different ways. But one things for sure, NOBODY who survives a deployment like that comes back the same person. Every time something bad happened, its like I left a little piece of me there with it. Only to be replaced with the horrible memories. Shit happened to us on a daily basis. It wasn't one particular event that really affected our minds. It was the day in and day out of constant bullshit. It was never feeling safe and secure throughout the entire deployment. We were always on edge, living every day like today was going to be the last day on earth. Month after month of feeling like that, really is what warps our brains. Like I said before, it was a grind. Not one time did we feel safe. Not one time did we feel good about anything. That, is what our PTSD is coming from. And add on top of that specific events that we witnessed, it becomes unbearable. When I tell you its constantly on our minds 24-7 that's not an exaggeration, like a video loop that plays over and over nonstop. I've seen my friends get killed ten thousand times in my head. Along with all the other shit too. Its like a thunderstorm that constantly rolls through your head, and its always raining. There's no escaping it. And its something that seemingly won't ever go away either. We lash out in extreme anger over the smallest issues and sometimes we sink into a deep depression that seems impossible to bounce back from. I have actually isolated myself from my friends and family because of this. Just falling asleep at night becomes an overwhelming task. Our heads are flooded with our memories and we seemingly can never turn it off. It's a constant feeling of drowning, im treading water but I cant quite keep my face above the water. Some of us experience the pain right off the bat. For me personally, things got harder as the years passed. Last year being my hardest year by far. One thing that I have learned though is what we go through is completely normal. We as humans aren't made to see the horrible things that we saw, we just aren't. Sure we had our training to prepare us for those situations, and when the time came we kicked ass and performed like Marines. But all that training was about how to turn that switch on. Turning that switch off is where we struggle. In country, ive have never been so close to God and the devil all at the same time. In order to defeat evil, you have to become more evil than the enemy who is trying to kill you. We looked to God to ask for our protection, and we looked to the devil to fight with a warrior rage. But now we're back home and that switch never quite turned off. And its something that we will have to cope with for the rest of our lives. The fucked up part about it, is its something that I never want to forget. Somehow when I sit back and think about it all, I find comfort. As much as it haunts me, I don't want it to leave me. Its who I am now. Its what makes me the person I am today. I think that's the hardest part with combat veterans. Trying to let go of the past, but the past wont let go of us. And even if we could forget about it, we don't really want to. So for me its about accepting that it will always be there, and learning how to cope with it. For our family members that are trying understand things... stop. Because you won't . The best thing you can do is ask about it. Engage in it. Don't worry about opening up something with them that they are trying to forget. Its impossible for us to forget. Its always there, always has been there, and always will be there. So its not like your reminding us about a painful time. Its always a painful time. One of the hardest things for us is realizing that nobody cares anymore. Not that it's the truth by any means, but its how we perceive it. Families tend to ignore it because they don't want us get back to a dark place, but we see it as nobody cares about it anymore. The ugly truth is when we got home, the war ended for our families. But for us, the war is just beginning. Even if you ask us about it, we still might not be ready to talk about it. But knowing that we still have people that care, means the world to us. The rest of this chapter I want to share my own experiences and things ive done to somewhat pull myself out of the slump. Don't get me wrong, im still learning. But hopefully someone reading this will take something positive away and make a change for the better. I wrote the following statement last year in probably my lowest point, these words will remain true till the day I die. "Our hearts are worn out. We have seen the horrors of battle. We have heard the cries of their families. And we have heard the sound of Taps far too many damn times. Let us remember the good times. Let us remember the men they were. Let us thank God we had the privilege serving with these warriors. But its time we start living again too. Live For Them."

Since we came home from our 2005 deployment, we have lost six Marines from our platoon from suicide due to PTSD. Six, out of roughly thrity five that we came home with. I get told by so many people when these things happen. "I just cant understand how someone could do that to themselves, how someone could take their own life." Or "I don't care how bad it gets I would never do that". So I thought maybe I could put things into perspective. The best way I can explain any of this to people is by metaphor. I look at all of our lives as a cup. Empty cup, everything is great with absolutely no problems. A full cup means we're at our max, our boiling point. Game over. For veterans who have experienced combat like this, our cup stays half full. Maybe even more. And that's just combat related experiences/problems. That's not including ANY other life problems. Which we all know life is full of problems. That's why when anything else is added to our cup it becomes overwhelming. That's what triggers the anger or even worse we shutdown with depression.

And this is something that seemingly will never go away. That's why its so easy for our cup to get full. And once your cup is full, and you're in that low point, there is nothing else on your mind. Not family, not friends, not help, nothing...........but that. We all have our low points, its just sometimes some of us reach a point that's a little bit lower. And in that moment its so easy to make a permanent decision for a tempo-rary state of mind. I've had many low points throughout the years, but my lowest was last year. I remember leaving work heading home. I was already a little down because we were coming up on our anniversary dates from the deployment. And as those dates get closer my anxiety peaks. I really cant describe the feeling I had when I left work that day other than this, it was like a wave of darkness that hit me all at once. The whole way home it got darker. Until the point where I pulled off the road into a parking lot. The whole world collapsed in on me. I sat there for about forty five minutes with a pistol in my hand. Nothing else was on my mind. Suicide was the only thing that seemed right at the time, it seemed like that was the only way I would ever release my demons and find peace. Somehow, by God's good grace, that darkness started fading away and I started feeling better and went on home. That was the darkest forty five minutes of my life. There are so many other veterans that experience something similar. Its not that we're crazy, its just our reality. In those really dark moments that's the only thing that makes sense to us. And even though we understand, its frustrating as hell to us when we find out about our brothers taking their lives. Its like a little part of us dies with them. And all we can think about is how much they had to live for, and how much better of a life they could have had. And how things could have been different if we just reached out a little more often. It haunts us daily and always will.

In my experiences, these are a few things that have helped me rebuild my life. These may not work for you, but if nothing else it's a good starting point.

1. Go to the VA. I fought it for years and years. I didn't want to go for two reasons. I didn't feel like I deserved it. I have a

brother that's missing an arm and one that is paralyzed from the waist down. I always felt like those people deserved it, not me. I didn't want to get into the system. Somehow I felt like I would be taking away from those who deserve it more. My second reason for not going is because I didn't want to talk to some old doctor about my experiences that has no fucking clue what im talking about. I just figured it was pointless. The last thing I wanted was for them to nod their head at my stories, throw some pills at me, and say good luck fucker. Well im here to say that its all bullshit. Go to the VA. Even if you don't think you need to, go anyway. Get enrolled. It took me right at a year and a half from when I submitted my paperwork until I finally sat down with a psychiatrist. Im not at all about to tell you how wonderful the VA is, it flat out sucks. But I do believe it's a necessary evil. And there are people there who genuinely do care. I got lucky and had an awesome nurse and doctor. Its just the system in general is horribly slow. It takes months to get anything scheduled, and that's if you can get anybody on the phone. Thats the number one issue I have with the VA. When a veteran comes to terms that he/she needs help, the help needs to be instant. Not a year from then. So that's why I say get enrolled now so that when you do need it, itll be a much easier process. I found the best use of the VA was for the meds. At the time I went, I really needed something to take the edge off. Its not a permanent fix, its just a start in the right direction. Don't expect to get much counseling out of the VA though. Scheduling to see a therapist was a six month wait. What the hell is the point in that, what good is that going to do? The VA has other options for counseling if you need it. At least where I live we have the Vet Center. Its funded by the VA, but they're two separate businesses. I highly recommend that if you can locate one nearby. There you'll be able to see a counselor once a week if needed. That's where youll learn better how to cope with PTSD.

2. Don't let yourself get to those low moments. When you feel that wave of darkness beginning to take over, do something right then to take your mind off of it. Don't let it set in and pull you in a downward spiral. Learn what works best for you. For me its music. When I start to feel it, I put my headphones in and calm myself down. Its easier said than done, but it does work. And that very well could be the biggest factor in saving your life. Music also helps me fall asleep at night. Somehow it drowns out the pain and lets my head relax.

3. Get tattoos. This one is self-explanatory. Its actually been proven that tattoos help veterans cope with their PTSD much easier. Maybe so, or maybe its just an excuse for me to go get another one. Either way I feel much better when I do. Most of mine have a deep meaning behind them that reminds me of something I went through, or still going through. It gives me strength sometimes when im at a low point to look down at them and remember why I have them. It reminds me of a time that tried to break me, but didn't.

4. Find a hobby. If im not actively doing something im thinking about Iraq. The busier I am with hobbies the less my mind is flooded with all the shit from over there. Get in the garage and build something, go to the shooting range, play sports, lift weights, anything. Just stay active.

5. Link up with your fellow brothers. This one is probably the most important one. There is no better therapy than to meet up with guys in your platoon and bullshit with them. Things that are hard to think about and almost impossible to talk to anyone about, you can laugh about with those guys. I went

about ten years before I linked up with my guys. Its not easy to do for some reason, before we met up the first time my anxiety was through the roof and I almost didn't want to go. But the first second we linked up, we picked up right where we left off ten years before. Its like we never missed a beat. Now several of us try to get together every few months or so. Words cant describe how it is when im with my brothers, all I know is im happiest when im around them.

Even with all the bad memories over there, I probably have just as many good ones too. I've had the worst days and the best days of my life in Iraq. Theres no better feeling than rolling into a town in an armored convoy geared up with all of your brothers ready to fight. And afterwards leaving a firefight when you've kicked ass and took names and are still alive, you feel like a God. Theres no better adrenaline rush than surviving something that should have killed you, but didn't. And theres nothing that warms my heart more than seeing a mangled up dead muj motherfucker. But most important, theres no better feeling than fighting side by side with your brothers. I think that's what we all miss the most. Its each other. That's the main reason we fight anyway, for the men next to us. That's why its so hard coming back home because there isn't that brotherhood anymore, not like overseas. That's why most of us yearn to be back over there. If given the opportunity to go back we would in a heartbeat. Not to chase the glory, because those of us who have been there know that there is no glory in war. Its about the brotherhood. Its about being amongst people who were stripped down to the core and performed at their best. Life, while harder, was much simpler over there. Protect each other. While he's on watch, I can sleep. It's a simple code, but it creates a bond that nothing else could replace. Sometimes it feels like ive peaked in life, like my best days are behind me. I think that a lot of us share that exact same feeling. Its like we're pitbulls on a leash, praying for shit to hit the fan just so we could kick ass and feel alive again. We are warriors. Its who we are now. We once stood toe to toe with some of the most evil mother fuckers on this planet, and won. That's something to be proud of. But life doesn't have to end for us there. I don't want to spend the rest of my life knowing that my best days are behind me and if I keep believing that, it will remain true until I die. Instead I want to believe that my best days are yet to come. That's what gives me that drive to keep pushing forward.

PTSD is something that we will have for the rest of our lives. But we don't need to look at it as a bad thing or a sign of weakness. Instead we should look at it as a badge of honor. Its something we have earned and we should wear it with pride. As the saying goes, "Its hard to let go of the demons inside. They were holding you when no one else would." Truer words have never been spoken. But we should learn to embrace those demons, not let it consume our lives. Our scars tell a story about us, about a time when the greatest men in the world stood side by side and did the impossible. Instead of letting it eat away at us, we should turn it into something positive. Let's let our war define us, not our pain. Live For Them. Its what our fallen brothers would want for us. Keep their spirits alive by living ourselves. Never give up warriors, NEVER.

Keep Pushing Forward.

Semper Fi.

May 17, 2023

It is now 18 years since combat, anniversary date of Davis and Coles mortar day, 5 years since I have written the previous in this chapter. Not much has changed, but a lot has changed. I now live in a world that I feel completely alone in. anywhere I go in public, I feel so completely isolated. I look around at people and see so many that have absolutely no idea what I have seen and am going through. In a room full of people, im alone. I am realizing that this will never leave me. I am realizing what our Vietnam veterans are still going through right now. I more understand that this will never leave me. It does me good to go back and read what I have written before, just in this chapter. Its not about trying to get over it, its about trying to cope with it. But even that becomes a huge task for some of us sometimes. I am writing this now, since the last time I wrote, now lost my wife and family, lost my job, lost my sanity, lost my purpose. But I stand here before you, that I have NOT lost my way. Even though now, in all my years, this is the worst part of my life. The water is still around my face like I am drowning, and can hardly catch my breath. But, I am still here. I am still treading water. One thing I will say after all these years, is actually listing the number 6 on my list.

6. Write your experiences down. Weather its in a journal, having rough nights, feeling hopeless, anniversary dates, etc. Write your feelings down and write down your memories. I promise you it will pay you back in the present, and also pay you back in the future, like its doing for me right now. It's a good reminder for all of us to remember who we once were, and to go forward in life continuing on as the warriors that we once were before then. It'll give you a sense of hope and encouragement to Keep Pushing Forward. Also, another thing that has kept me moving, is making our thoughts and emotions public. Get your story out!!! I continuously post on Facebook anniversary dates and remember our brothers. I have been overwhelmingly welcomed by friends and family members of the ones that we lost come to me and thanking me for writing about how their loved one died. Or fellow veterans come to me saying "Thank you so much for saying that, I went through something similar and nobody understands." It reaches home to more veterans and reaches the heart of more than you can imagine. Just today, which made me to update this chapter, I posted on facebook the anniversary date of them getting hit with a mortar. A fellow brother of mine in a local bar came to me about the post. Vietnam veteran Mr Howard Burgess said to me that after reading my post he immediately thought about a similar experience that he had. And he thanked me for sharing that. Which only tells me that there's more of us out there than we think, and the more we share with each other, the more all of us feel normal.

Ultimately, most of us at this point, just want to feel normal. Like were not freaks. Its something we can bond with us few and can comfort our hearts. "Let your story go! Let your heart flow! Tell them your story that you have never told before. Unpack the demons. Unleash your heart and mind. You will feel comfort, more than you never knew before". – Jason Teed.

I want to leave this book with one thing. What its like to be a veteran. I wrote this just a few months ago, hoping to open the communication between veterans and loved ones. This is 100% from my heart soul. Its my heart pouring out to all of yall.......

WHAT DOES IT MEAN TO BE A VETERAN

Yes, we signed the dotted line (which honestly, I don't think it was dotted, just a regular line) yes we wrote a blank check blah blah blah. But why did we do it?

We did it because we felt like it was right.

We knew the importance.

We didn't care about having a college party life.

We wanted to serve our beautiful country.

We were willing to die for our country.

We wanted to carry traditions of our family and founders.

We wanted to ensure the freedom of our country.

We stood up, when everyone sat down.

We wanted our unborn kids to live happily and free.

We wanted to make you proud.

We understood the sacrifices.

We understood the risks.

We were willing to go endless amounts of time without sleeping, endless training, in the mud, war, trading bullets, starv-
ing, wore out, sometimes hopeless, but still Pushing Forward.

We were willing to live an entire lifetime with this weighing
in our minds.

We were willing to give up everything we know, everything
we own, everything we have, just so that we see our nation
survive.

We were willing to give all that up for YOU.

We were an instrument, under God's eye, to carry out what is
necessary.

We were the line of defense that stands between you and the
enemy.

We didn't know what was to happen with us, but did it anyway.

We care.

We love all of you.

And we all realized this at a very early age.

In short, we did all of that so that our loved ones didn't have to.

We did this........for you.

What makes us special? Nothing. It's just who we are. It's what we were supposed to be. It's what we were born to do.

What does it mean to be a veteran? Everything. Our entire lives. And we wouldn't trade it for the world.

God Bless the ones who stood up, when others didn't. God Bless our warriors.

God Bless everyone who wore a uniform. And above all else, God Bless our country.

Because of that.....we are still free!
Semper Fi.....Always Faithful

"THE PATH OF A SURVIVING COMBAT WARRIOR"

JASON TEED

The path of a surviving combat warrior.

Not knowing what your purpose in life is.

Not knowing why your brothers died, and you lived.

Not knowing how to let go of the fallen, because the last time you saw them was on the battle field. And no closure for any of it.

Not being able to enjoy any holiday or even your birthday because of survivors guilt.

Not wanting to live.

Not trusting in God that there's a reason you're still here, because of not seeing it.

Not trusting in people other than your fellow warriors.

Not believing that things will get better.

Not seeing happiness, but can't unsee your friends blood soaked cammies.

Not understanding the innocent that you have seen dead, including children.

Not understanding the lives you had to take.

Not knowing if you're going to live throughout the day. And feeling that way every single hour, every single day for many months on end.

Not eating enough, but still giving to the ones in need.

Not sleeping.

Pulling your brothers out of burning rubble.

Never feeling safe.

Seeing your brothers fall.

Hearing your brother's cries. And NEVER forgetting it.

Hearing the mortars, rpg's, and rounds coming in.

Hearing your vehicle getting hit with rounds.

Living through a bomb.

Living through multiple mortar attacks, even when your brothers were wounded.

Thinking the last letter you wrote home, is the last of your own words.

Writing your own will, not notarized, but trusting your brother will take care of it.

Trusting in your brothers. Watching over him while he sleeps, and trusting in him while you sleep.

Hearing the evil sounds from within the cities.

Fighting.

Killing.

Smelling burning flesh.

The smell of your brothers blood.

Smelling enemy gun powder, because you were that close.

Smelling war.... and never forgetting it.

Cleaning up body parts.

Not feeling needed anymore.

Not feeling worthy anymore.

Not feeling wanted anymore unless someone needs something.

Providing freedom for people that don't care, give a shit, or take advantage of.

But never giving up on people.

Upholding your constitutional duty, to protect all people. And knowing that people aren't willing to do the same.

Knowing that you should have died several times over, but didn't. And living with that.

The surviving warriors way. Too many questions to answer. Too much to comprehend. Too much to fathom. Too much to put on our shoulders. Never getting the help or support we need from the government, even though we gave everything we had for them and our country. Our brains are so tired. Our souls are so depleted. Our hearts are dead.

And on top of all of that, still having to shoulder normal everyday life problems, with everyday issues, normal life depression, normal life stress.

Yep, the true surviving Warriors path.

ALL GAVE SOME
48 GAVE ALL

Sgt. Bradley Harper
Cpl. David Stewart
Lcpl. Kevin Waruinge
Sgt. David Kreuter
Lcpl. William Wightman
Sgt. Justin Hoffman
Lcpl. Aaron Reed
Sgt. David Wimberg
Lcpl. Nicholas Erdy
Cpl. Andre Williams
Lcpl. Grant Fraser
Lcpl. Chris Dyer
Ssgt. Kendall Ivy II
Lcpl. Jourdan Grez
Lcpl. Nicholas Bloem
Lcpl. Timothy Bell Jr
Lcpl. Edward Schroeder II
Lcpl. Christopher Lyons
Pfc. Christopher Dixon
Sgt. Michael Marzano
HM3 Jeffery Wiener
Maj. Ricardo Crocker
Lcpl. Dustin Birch
Lcpl. Daniel Chavez

Lcpl. Michael Cifuentes
Cpl. Dustin Derga
HM3 Travis Youngblood
Ssgt. Anthony Goodwin
Lcpl. Jonathan Grant
Lcpl. Eric Bernholtz
Lcpl. Wesley Davids
Lcpl. Thomas Keeling
Lcpl. Devon Seymour
Cpl. Brad Squires
Ssgt. Josheph Goodrich
Lcpl. Ryan Kovacicek
Sgt. Nathaniel Rock
Cpl. Jeffrey Boskovich
Lcpl. Roger Castleberry Jr
Sgt. David Coullard
Lcpl. Daniel Deyarmin
Sgt. James Graham III
Lcpl. Brian Montgomery
Cpl. Bryan Richardson
Cpl. Michael Lindemuth
Cpl. Joseph Tremblay
Sgt. Aaron Cepeda
Lcpl. Lance Graham

I would LOVE to give credit to someone who is very special to me. Without her none of this would be possible. Thank you so much Kim Murphy Orr!! Love you always!

Printed in the USA
CPSIA information can be obtained
at www.ICGtesting.com
LVHW061942090324
773952LV00017B/417

9 781649 906496